The Book of
ICHIGO ICHIE

The Book of
ICHIGO
ICHIE

The Art of Making the Most of
Every Moment, the Japanese Way

HÉCTOR GARCÍA
AND
FRANCESC MIRALLES

Translated by Charlotte Whittle

Quercus

First published in 2019 in the United States by Penguin Books, an imprint of
Penguin Random House LLC

First published in Great Britain in 2019 by

Quercus Editions Ltd
Carmelite House
50 Victoria Embankment
London EC4Y 0DZ

An Hachette UK company

A CIP catalogue record for this book is available
from the British Library.

HB ISBN 978 1 52940 129 5
Ebook ISBN 978 1 52940 132 5

Originally published in Spanish as *Ichigo-Ichie: El arte japonés de vivir momentos inolvidables*

By Penguin random House Grupo Editorial, Barcelona, 2019

Image credits: p. 21: "The Sumida Embankment in the Eastern Capital" from Hiroshige's
Thirty- six Views of Mount Fuji woodblock print series (1858), via Wikimedia Commons; p. 29 and
p. 186: © Héctor García and Francesc Miralles; p. 53: Image by Mohamed Hassan, via Pixabay.
p. 101: Courtesy of Phil Libin. All rights reserved. p. 106: Woodblock print from Toshikata
Mizuno's *A Tea Ceremony Periwinkle* series (1897), via Wikimedia Commons. p. 137: Adapted
from an image by MesserWoland, via Wikimedia Commons.

10 9 8 7 6 5 4 3 2 1

Book design by Lucia Bernard

Printed and bound in Great Britain by Clays Ltd, Elcograf S.p.A.

Before beginning to study the sacred texts and constantly

singing the sutras, the student should learn to read

the love letters sent by the snow, the wind, and the rain.

—IKKYŪ, Zen master

CONTENTS

PROLOGUE: IN AN OLD TEAROOM ··· *1*

ICHIGO ICHIE ··· *5*

Part I: The Beauty of Impermanence

Kaika and *Mankai* ··· *19*

And You, Where Do You Live? ··· *35*

Zensations ··· *51*

Dukkha and *Mono No Aware* ··· *63*

Destiny Depends on a Moment ··· *77*

Part II: Living *Ichigo Ichie*

The Ceremony of Attention · · · *95*

The Art of Listening · · · *113*

The Art of Looking · · · *121*

The Art of Touching · · · *127*

The Art of Tasting · · · *133*

The Art of Smelling · · · *139*

Part III: The Little School of *Ichigo Ichie*

The Art of Parties · · · *147*

Collective Mindfulness · · · *159*

Returning to Now · · · *169*

What If . . . ? · · · *181*

The *Ichigo Ichie* Formula · · · *185*

Epilogue: The Ten Rules of *Ichigo Ichie* · · · *189*

ACKNOWLEDGMENTS · · · *193*

SUGGESTIONS FOR FURTHER READING · · · *195*

The Book of
ICHIGO ICHIE

Prologue: In an Old Tearoom

On the afternoon that, though we didn't yet know it, this book was about to be born, a storm was battering the narrow streets of Gion, in the heart of Kyoto—home of the last remaining geishas, among other mysteries. We found refuge in a *chashitsu*, a teahouse, which was empty because of the downpour.

Sitting at a low table beside the window, we noticed that the torrent of water rushing down the narrow street was sweeping with it *sakura* petals from blossoming cherry trees.

Spring had sprung and summer was on its way, and soon nothing would be left of those white petals that inspired such passion in the Japanese.

An elderly woman in a kimono asked us what we would like, and we chose the most special variety of tea on the menu—a *gyokuro* from Ureshino, a place in the south of Japan where the best tea in the world is said to be grown.

As we waited for the steaming teapot and the cups to arrive, we shared our impressions of Japan's former capital. We were amazed that there were two thousand temples in the hills surrounding the city, whose population is smaller than that of Philadelphia.

Then we listened in silence to the rain pounding the cobblestones.

When the old woman returned with the tray, the tea's fragrant aroma roused us from that brief and pleasant torpor. We lifted our cups to see the bright green infusion before savoring the first sip, which tasted both bitter and sweet.

At that very moment, a young woman riding a bicycle while holding an umbrella passed by the old teahouse and smiled shyly at us before disappearing into a narrow street.

It was then that we each looked up and discovered the wooden plaque on a dark brown pillar. It bore this inscription:

一期一会

We set about deciphering those characters, pronounced "*ichigo ichie*," while the damp wind swayed a small bell hanging from the eaves of the teahouse, making it ring. The meaning of *ichigo ichie* is something like this: *What we are experiencing right now will never happen again.* And therefore, we must value each moment like a beautiful treasure.

This message perfectly describes what we experienced that rainy afternoon in Kyoto's old town.

We began to talk of other unique, unrepeatable moments like that one, to which perhaps we hadn't paid enough attention because we were too concerned with the past, the future, or the distractions of the present.

A student walking through the rain, carrying a backpack and fiddling with his cell phone, provided a clear example of the latter and reminded us of a quote by Henry David Thoreau: "As if you could kill time without injuring eternity."

That spring afternoon, in a sudden flash of inspiration, we understood something that gave us food for thought in the months to come. In our age of complete distraction and our culture of instant gratification, when we often fail to listen, and engage only superficially with our surroundings, each person contains a key that can open the door to attention, harmony with others, and love of life.

And that key is called *ichigo ichie*.

In the pages that follow, we will share a unique and transformative experience, discovering how to make each and every instant the best moment of our lives.

Héctor García and Francesc Miralles

Ichigo Ichie

The Japanese characters that make up this book's central concept don't have an exact equivalent in English, but let's look at two interpretations that will help us to understand them.

Ichigo ichie can be translated as "Once, a meeting" and also as "In this moment, an opportunity." What this means to tell us is that each meeting, everything we experience, is a unique treasure that will never be repeated in the same way again. So if we let it slip away without enjoying it, the moment will be lost forever.

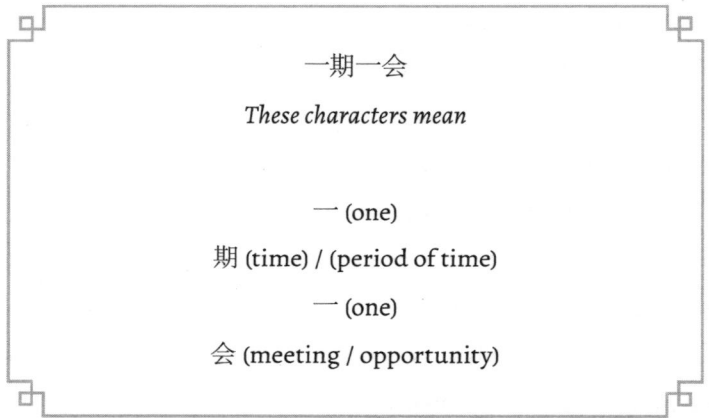

一期一会

These characters mean

一 (one)

期 (time) / (period of time)

一 (one)

会 (meeting / opportunity)

The Gates of Shambhala

A Tibetan legend illustrates this concept very clearly. The story goes that a hunter was pursuing a deer across the frozen peaks of the Himalayas when he came upon an enormous mountain split in two, allowing him to see what was on the other side.

Beside the opening in the mountain, an old man with a long beard beckoned to the startled hunter to come closer and see.

The hunter obeyed and peered into the vertical crack

that was just wide enough for one man to pass through. What he saw left him breathless.

On the other side of the opening was a fertile garden, bathed in sunlight and seeming to go on forever. Children played happily among trees laden with fruit, and animals frolicked freely in a world filled with beauty, serenity, and abundance.

"Do you like what you see?" the old man asked when he saw the hunter's amazement.

"Of course I like it . . . this must be paradise!"

"Indeed, it is, and you have found it. Why don't you come in? Here, you can live happily ever after."

Overflowing with joy, the hunter answered, "I will, but first I want to go find my brothers and friends. I'll come back with them soon."

"As you wish. But remember, the gates of Shambhala open only once in a lifetime," the old man warned him, frowning slightly.

"I won't be long," said the hunter, before running off.

Excited by what he'd just seen, he retraced the path he had taken, crossing valleys, rivers, and hills until he reached his village, where he told his two brothers and three childhood friends of his discovery.

The group set out at a brisk pace, guided by the hunter, and before the sun dipped below the horizon, they managed to reach the high mountain that gave access to Shambhala.

But the mountain pass had closed, never to open again.

The man who had discovered that miraculous world would keep hunting for the rest of his life.

Now or Never

The first part of the term *ichigo ichie* (一期) is used in Buddhist scripture to refer to the time that passes from the moment we are born until we die. As we have just seen in the Tibetan legend, the opportunity or encounter with life is what is offered to you now. If you don't seize the moment, it will be lost forever.

As the well-known saying goes, you only live once. Each unique, unrepeatable moment is an open gate to Shambhala, and there will never be a second chance to walk through it.

This is something we all know as human beings but easily forget when we allow ourselves to get caught up in our everyday worries and obligations.

Becoming aware of *ichigo ichie* helps us take our foot off the gas and remember that each morning we spend in the world, every moment we spend with our children and with our loved ones is infinitely valuable and deserves our full attention.

This is the case, first and foremost, because we don't know when life will end. Each day could be our last. No one can be sure when they go to sleep that they will open their eyes again the next morning.

There is a monastery in Spain where it is said that whenever the monks run into each other in the passageway, they say to each other, "Brother, remember that one day you're going to die." This custom places them in a permanent now, which, far from causing them sadness or worry, inspires them to enjoy every moment of their lives.

As Marcus Aurelius writes in his *Meditations*, the drama of existence is not death but *never having begun to live*.

Ichigo ichie is a clear invitation to "now or never," since though we may manage to live many years, every meeting has a unique essence and will never be repeated.

Perhaps we'll run into the same people in the same place again, but we'll be older, our situation and our humor will be distinct; we'll be carrying the weight of other priorities and other experiences. The universe is in a constant state of flux, and so are we. That's why nothing will ever happen again in the same way.

The Origins of the Term

The first written example we have of *ichigo ichie* is in a notebook belonging to the tea master Yamanoue Sōji, in 1588. What he wrote was this:

> Treat your host as if the meeting were going to occur only once in your life.

If we leave the Japanese term in question untranslated, we could phrase the command like this: "Treat your host with *ichigo ichie*."

When Yamanoue Sōji included this phrase in his

notes, he was writing about what he had learned from the tea ceremony under the tutelage of the tea master Rikyū, considered one of the founders of *wabi-cha*, a style of tea ceremony that emphasizes simplicity above all else.

However, to express this concept, Sōji turned to old Japanese, using 一期一度, which is almost the same as the original, 一期一会, but with a different last character, which means "time" rather than "meeting."

The change is important, since it allows us to understand the unique character of each moment beyond the tea ceremony—to which we're going to dedicate a whole chapter in order to understand its philosophical depth.

THE TIME IS NOW

Each tea ceremony should be treated with great attention because it is *ichigo ichie*, which is to say, a unique encounter in time. Even though the host and guests may see each other daily, the gathering can never be exactly repeated.

If we consider the extraordinary nature of every moment, we realize that each encounter is a once-in-a-lifetime occasion.

The host should thus show true sincerity and take the greatest care with every detail, to make sure that everything flows smoothly and without a hitch.

The guests for their part must understand that the encounter will never occur again, and so they must appreciate every detail of the ceremony prepared by the host and, of course, participate wholeheartedly.

All this is what is meant by the expression "*ichigo ichie*."

—Ii Naosuke, "Great Elder" of the Tokugawa Shogunate, in *Chanoyu ichi-e shu* (1858)

Current Usage of *Ichigo Ichie*

Beyond the tea ceremony setting, today the Japanese use the expression *ichigo ichie* in two situations:

1. When meeting a stranger for the first time.
2. When meeting acquaintances, to emphasize that every occasion is unique.

For example, imagine you are lost in the streets of Kyoto, and when you ask for help, you end up chatting for ten minutes because the person you asked for directions happens to have lived in the United States for a while. When you part company, *ichigo ichie* would be an appropriate way to say goodbye. By saying this, you let them know that this was a pleasant encounter that will not happen again in the future.

The second usage is closer to what we've seen with the tea ceremony. It's used with friends we see often, to emphasize that each time we meet is unique and special. Our lives go on, and each of us grows and is transformed as time goes by. As Heraclitus said, "No man ever steps in the same river twice, for it's not the same river and he's not the same man."

In both uses of the expression, the point is to show gratitude and appreciate a shared moment in our lives. At the same time, it also conveys a hint of nostalgia, and like the ritual of the monks mentioned earlier, it reminds us that our passage through life is fleeting. *Ichigo ichie* makes us aware that each time could be the last.

Hunting Moments

The goal of this book is not only to introduce you to the many fascinating aspects of Japanese culture related to *ichigo ichie* but also to help you create and experience unforgettable moments, with yourself and with others.

As you'll see in the chapters that follow, the cultivation and practice of *ichigo ichie* will allow you to lead a happier, more fulfilled life, without feeling weighed down by the past or anxious about the future. You will learn to live fully in the present, acknowledging and appreciating the gift of every moment.

At the end of this journey together, we will have become hunters of special moments. We will know how to capture these moments mid-flight, and savor them for what they are: unique, once-in-a-lifetime experiences.

There's a *Peanuts* cartoon that shows Snoopy and

Charlie Brown from behind, sitting on a jetty beside a lake, having the following conversation:

"Someday, we will all die, Snoopy!"

"True, but on all the other days, we will not."

The meaning of the second statement goes beyond humor. We don't know when we'll have to leave this world—and that's just as well—but what does depend on us is how we spend "all the other days," all those when we are alive. And those days are made up of encounters and moments that we can either allow to slip away or make unforgettable.

This reminds us of the end of the epic film *Boyhood*, which Richard Linklater filmed with the same actors over the course of twelve years so that the viewer could see life pass by before his eyes. For 165 minutes, we watch Mason—who at the beginning of the film is a boy of six whose parents are divorced—as he grows up and has a range of experiences, until he starts college.

After Mason overcomes many difficulties, the film ends with him going on a hiking trip with his new college friends. Mason has become an intelligent, sensitive young man, and he watches the sun set with a girl we suspect will become important in his life.

"You know how everyone's always saying 'seize the moment'?" she says excitedly. "I don't know, I'm kinda thinkin' it's the other way round. You know, like, *the moment seizes us.*"

The meaning of this scene has been widely discussed, and it has much to do with *ichigo ichie.*

Just as pregnant women see baby bumps everywhere they look, as soon as we become moment hunters, everything ends up being unique and sublime, since we have the privilege of knowing that *what we are experiencing right now will never happen again.*

Part I

The Beauty of
Impermanence

Kaika and *Mankai*

Those familiar with the Land of the Rising Sun know that the most beautiful days of the year are when the *sakura*, or Japanese cherry trees, blossom in springtime.

On the subtropical islands of Okinawa, where we conducted our research for our book about *ikigai*,* the *sakura* blossom in January. In Japan's large cities, the flowers can be seen between the end of March and the middle of April. And on the cold northern island of Hokkaido, the blossoming of the flowers is delayed until May.

Every year, the Japanese follow the *sakura* forecast keenly to know when the flowers will show their white

---

* "Reason for being" in Japanese, or, translated more freely, "the happiness of always being busy." We explore this concept in depth in *Ikigai: The Japanese Secret to a Long and Happy Life.*

petals, which are treasured not only for their beauty but also for their important symbolism, as we will see later in this chapter. The "cherry blossom front," as it is known, moves from south to north; each city has a special tree to announce the beginning of what has become a nature festival in which the entire country takes part.

In Japan there are ninety-six of these special "sample" trees. In Kyoto, for example, the tree can be found in the garden of the city's meteorological office. Each morning, an employee goes outside to see if the buds have opened. The day this happens, the news spreads across the whole country.

Hanami

When the blossom forecast, known as the *sakura zensen*, is fulfilled, the Japanese immediately crowd the country's parks for the ritual of *hanami*, which literally means "viewing the flowers."

If you visit a park or garden during this time, you'll find entire groups of office workers under the blossoming cherry trees, families enjoying a walk together, and couples taking pictures of each other with *sakura* in the background.

This celebration of nature and the renewal of life—and hope—is so long-standing a tradition that records of *hanami* festivals date back to the third century.

After the sun goes down, the celebration continues with what is known as *yozakura,* or "night cherry blossom." At dusk, traditional lanterns that hang from the trees are lit, giving the parks and gardens the magical atmosphere of a Studio Ghibli film.

Groups of friends and couples sit beneath the blossoms at night, with a glass of sake and some snacks to enjoy the moment. This is undoubtedly an *ichigo ichie* experience, since when the petals fall in a couple of weeks, they will have to wait a whole year to experience it again—with luck, if they are still here.

Sakura is visible proof of how the most beautiful things in life are fleeting and can't be postponed.

The cherry blossom celebration officially begins with *kaika*, a term that refers to the earliest buds. The flower opens completely after a week, reaching the state known as *mankai*, which means "the exact moment when the *sakura* flower is fully opened."

A week later the cherry blossom's petals begin to fall. This can happen earlier, caused by wind or rain, like during our visit to Kyoto's old town.

The Japanese enjoy this moment, too. They even have a word, *hanafubuki*, to describe a flurry of *sakura* petals, a sublime moment that expresses the beauty and poetry of the impermanent.

The Magic of the *Kaika*

Hikari Oe, the severely disabled son of the Nobel Prize-winning writer Kenzaburo Oe, discovered music while strolling through a park with his parents, when he heard—and began to imitate—the sound of birdsong.

This is a typical *kaika* moment, when something unknown begins to blossom within us.

There is a kind of magic whenever a new passion is sparked, though it often arises in unmagical places.

For example, Dan Brown says that it had never occurred to him to write until he came across a book that had been left behind in a hammock at a hotel swimming pool.

He had gone on a package vacation with his wife and he was bored, but the novel he found, *The Doomsday Conspiracy* by Sidney Sheldon, saved his vacation.

As soon as he got home, he decided that he, too, would write a thriller, and he immediately set about doing so, possessed by *kaika*. Years later, *The Da Vinci Code* was a worldwide bestseller, making him a millionaire.

Kaika is a strong presence when we fall in love, too. Like the cherry blossom that opens to announce the arrival of spring, someone who didn't even exist in our lives a moment before suddenly sweeps us off our feet, becoming our central focus.

In the mysterious realm of love, this blossoming can have the most unexpected effects. What makes us fall in love?

When we ask other people about that unforgettable moment when a whole new world opens up to us, they tell us things such as the following:

- "The first time I heard his voice, I felt breathless."
- "Her eyes, at once shy and penetrating, made me want to know what she was like inside."
- "I fell in love with the gentle way he cleaned up the mess I'd just made."

All of these are unique, *ichigo ichie* moments that, if we know how to seize and value them, can light up the rest of our lives.

The *Mankai* Formula

When *kaika* is transformative, we want to turn it into *mankai*. In other words, we want to make sure that what has been born inside us matures and unfolds to its full potential. *Mankai* occurs, for example, when:

- The person who falls in love decides to tend the garden of the relationship, on both good and bad days, to prevent it from withering;
- The aspiring author who, after having an idea for a book, follows a daily schedule to progress with her writing until it is finished;
- The entrepreneur who doesn't want his idea to be a flash in the pan constantly seeks ways to improve and innovate.

In discussions of the marathon required to turn an initial idea or vocation into something we excel at, we often hear about Malcolm Gladwell's 10,000-hour rule for progressing from *kaika* to *mankai*.

In his book *Outliers*, Gladwell demonstrates how, in his words, "ten thousand hours is the magic number of greatness," citing the following examples:

- Bill Gates started programming at the age of ten while in middle school in Seattle. Ten thousand hours later, he was causing a sensation in the world of information technology.

- The Beatles completed their ten thousand hours to greatness in the nightclubs of Hamburg, where they performed eight hours a day, before going back to the UK, where "Love Me Do" became a smash hit.

Gladwell's conclusion is that genius isn't enough; a great deal of effort and commitment are required for talent to be realized in all its brilliance.

SWORDSMITHS

The attention to detail and patience of the Japanese can be seen in all kinds of disciplines. One of the most well-known cases is the restaurant Sukiyabashi Jiro, which, despite its location in the Ginza metro station, is considered the best in the world. The owner's son had to practice for several decades before he was able to make a good *tamago* (a Japanese omelet used in sushi).

For many arts and traditions, there is no school where you can learn their secrets; the knowledge is transmitted from master to apprentice. This is especially true in the case of people who make *katanas* and other Japanese swords.

Currently there are three hundred active swordsmiths left in Japan, but only thirty make their living exclusively from their trade. Each of these swordsmiths has apprentices working under them, so that the art of making their swords will not be lost.

Swordsmithing isn't something you can learn from a book or by taking a class. To acquire this skill, you must spend at least ten years studying under one of the three hundred masters—much longer than it takes to earn a university degree.

Why is it so hard to forge a good *katana*? We won't go into the details here, but the process of smelting good steel is as complicated or more so than making a good sushi omelet.

One of the most prized features of steel is a low level of carbon content, which preserves the steel's properties. The best Japanese sword blades contain as little as 1 percent, and no more than 1.2 percent.

This low content is extremely difficult to achieve. The masters know intuitively when a blade has reached these levels, once it has spent three days in the fire, at a temperature of between 2,200 and 2,800 degrees.

The traditional Japanese sword symbolizes strength, perseverance, and simplicity, since there is nothing ornamental about it. Hence the determination to produce the best material and then to forge it with a hammer to achieve the greatest possible density.

A life lesson for the swordsmiths, considered national treasures in Japan, is to *eliminate the unnecessary to get to the essential*—that's where beauty and power lie. And that can be achieved only with patience and perseverance.

When Daniel Goleman, the author of *Emotional Intelligence*, and others argued that persistence doesn't guarantee anything, and that some fields require extraordinary innate talent, Gladwell responded:

"There is a lot of confusion about the 10,000-hour rule that I talk about in *Outliers*. It doesn't apply to sports. And practice isn't a SUFFICIENT condition for success. I could play chess for a hundred years and I'll never be a grand master. The point is simply that natural ability requires a huge investment of time in order to be made manifest."

If we translate this into Japanese terms, the first part of the formula is *ikigai*: discovering something we become passionate about and which also comes easily to us.

Once we've identified our mission, then comes *kaika*, which is sometimes the most difficult part: setting aside other people's demands to make room for our passion, allowing the reason we feel we were put on the earth to begin to blossom.

IKIGAI

+

KAIKA

+

TIME

=

MANKAI

The third thing is to stay on that path, to be patient and to keep dreaming, until we obtain *mankai*.

To sum it up, the formula goes like this: *ikigai* + *kaika* + time = *mankai*.

If we discover our talent, open ourselves up to it, and make it a priority in our lives, our passion will be able to develop, leading to our happiness and that of others.

It's Never Too Late to Bloom

When we think of beginning, of developing something new, often what comes to mind is a young person with their whole life ahead of them, but this is only a prejudice. We all have the ability to make a new start in life, regardless of age.

Even an elderly person can decide to wipe the slate clean and reinvent themselves, because they, too, have their *whole life* ahead of them. What matters isn't how many more years we might live but what we will do with the time we have left.

In Japan, people often make a completely fresh start at the end of their "official" working lives. People who have spent most of their lives in offices, attending to the needs of a company, take responsibility for their own lives. Like the old Jedis in the *Star Wars* movies, for as long as the Force is with them, they defy their age by doing what they had always dreamed of doing.

That's why it's common to see tour guides of eighty years or more in small train stations, volunteering their services to visitors, telling them about the local sights and offering advice on bus schedules and hiking opportunities.

For example, a traveler getting off at the station in Yudanaka, a town known for its *onsen*—hot springs—and the jumping-off point for visiting the Nagano snow monkeys, will be greeted on their arrival by these charming elderly guides, who are happy to be able to practice their English with travelers from all over the world.

As we learned from the masters of longevity in Okinawa during our research for *Ikigai*, if you're brave enough to do what you love, every day could be the best day of your life.

Two Examples of Late Bloomers

The term *late bloomer* is often used to describe someone who discovers her talent, perhaps even the *ikigai* that guides her in life, at a later age.

Defying the conventional wisdom that intellectual growth reaches its height in young adults and that once we reach maturity it declines with age, late bloomers never cease to improve and renew, always using the wisdom they have gained to take another step toward new challenges.

Here are two examples to prove that great achievements have no age limit.

The first is Melchora Aquino de Ramos, a woman from the Philippines who was eighty-four when the unrest broke out that would lead to her country's independence. Far from being intimidated, she used the shop she ran as a shelter for the wounded and persecuted, in addition to offering advice to the revolutionaries from those modest quarters where secret meetings were held.

The old woman's subversive activities came to the attention of the colonial authorities, who detained her and interrogated her about the identities of the revolutionary leaders. Melchora Aquino refused to give any information, and as a result she was deported to the Mariana Islands.

When the United States took control of the Philippines, Melchora returned home as a national heroine and was named "Grand Woman of the Revolution." She was actively involved in the creation of her new country for more than twenty years and died at the age of 107.

The arts are an even more fertile field for late bloomers. British-born Harry Bernstein published a short story at age twenty-four but would not begin his novel *The Invisible Wall* until he was ninety-three. He managed to finish it and witnessed its publication in 2007, at the age of ninety-six.

Bernstein was asked about his decision to write his debut novel so late in life. He explained that his loneliness after the loss of his wife, to whom he had been married for sixty-seven years, had motivated him.

Encouraged by his readers' response, Bernstein would write another three novels before his death at the age of 101. In addition to leaving this legacy, he said in an interview with *The New York Times*, "God knows what other potentials lurk in other people, if we could only keep them alive well into their nineties."

And You, Where Do You Live?

People who are able to lead a long and meaningful life usually have two characteristics: They are aware of their mission, and they know how to enjoy every moment. For them, the present moment is a permanent opportunity to experience *ichigo ichie*.

However, if we look at the people around us, or even at ourselves, we'll see that it's often difficult to stay in the present. Our thoughts wander in all directions, and it's hard to keep them focused on where we are now, on what we're doing now, and on whom we're with right now.

If you're alone, the person you're with is yourself.

The Four Basic Emotions and Time

There are four basic emotions—though the social psychologist Paul Ekman increased that to six, based on our facial expressions, to include surprise and disgust. They leave their mark on our lives and situate us in one place or another in time.

Let's take a look at each of them:

1. *Anger.* This emotion, linked to our survival instinct, originally helped us face danger that threatened us or our loved ones. That's why our muscles become tense when we get angry, preparing us to defend and counterattack, and our heartbeat gets faster. Our bodies produce adrenaline and noradrenaline, optimizing our response to stress but eventually leading to exhaustion.

In addition to being socially undesirable, the problem with anger is that it is rarely linked to any real threat, given that these days, except in extraordinary circumstances—when we find ourselves in a war zone or victims of a street attack—we have no predators.

Instead we get angry when we believe we are victims

of wrongdoing or when something that has happened to us is unfair. If we go on the attack, we often lose control and make the problem worse, since then the other party also feels threatened and attacks in turn. If we repress our rage, we can do ourselves harm.

Whether we attack or repress, anger is almost always a destructive emotion, as the Buddha taught: "Holding on to anger is like grasping a hot coal with the intent of throwing it at someone else: You are the one who gets burned."

When we get mad, it's almost always due to our interpretation of something that has happened or that someone has done. Therefore, *anger keeps us tied to the past*, preventing us from enjoying the here and now.

2. *Sadness*. This emotion often stems from a sense of loss, in a broad array of situations. We feel sadness when we lose a loved one to death or separation, and we go through a grieving process as we adjust to our new situation. We also feel sad when we lose a useful or valuable object—for instance, a cell phone—or when our car breaks down or our income is reduced.

There is also a more existential kind of sadness, which

invites us to reflect, such as when we lose hope or the will to live for no apparent reason and find ourselves in a state of apathy that leaves us diminished.

When this sadness lasts a long time, longer than is proportionate to the loss, it can lead to depression. When sadness is healthy, it allows us to understand what has happened, to say goodbye to what we loved, and to prepare a new strategy to move forward in life. It can be translated into art, in any form, as a path for our inner alchemy.

From a physiological point of view, Ekman points out that this emotion causes us to lower our eyelids and turn down our lips. A person who is sad doesn't pay attention to what's in front of them—they aren't in the present—and that's why we say that they have a "blank stare."

Sadness keeps us tied to the past because our attention is focused on what we lost, what no longer exists, or what we wanted but didn't get. In any case, as long as we're sad, we aren't in the here and now.

3. *Fear.* Just like anger, this emotion is closely connected to our survival instinct and serves to warn us of threats

or potential harm. When human beings lived in the jungle, fear was essential for detecting imminent danger and preparing our body to fight or flee.

As with anger, fear activates the secretion of adrenaline and noradrenaline, which cause our pulse and blood pressure to skyrocket, also making us hyperventilate. Other physical symptoms of fear include sweating, shaking, and muscle tension, which can sometimes make us feel paralyzed.

Just like with anger, the problem is that our fear alarm often goes off when no predator or real threat is present. We are afraid of things that might happen but that are not an immediate threat. We're afraid of losing our job, our partner, our friends' attention or affection, our health. . . .

When experienced on a sustained basis, this anticipatory fear, based on our predictions of what might happen, can lead to an anxiety disorder and even to panic attacks. Our fear is so great that we may even become paralyzed by fear of fear.

Fear is an emotion that projects us into the future. When we live in fear, it's impossible to enjoy what we do and what we have.

4. *Happiness*. This is the least studied emotion, and it has a mysterious character, since it isn't always justified, and some people have a special predisposition toward it, whereas others appear to sabotage it.

Depending on its intensity, happiness places us within a range of inner experiences, from serene contentment to uncontrolled euphoria. In all these cases, it's an emotion that conjures a celebration of life, lightheartedness, and optimism.

Happiness makes us effusive, which explains why, when we experience it, we want to share it with others. When we feel happy, we become more empathetic, generous, and human.

In a soccer match, after a player scores a goal, he runs toward his teammates to give them a hug. Happiness is something we experience and something we give. It not only puts us on the sunny side of life but also brings us closer to others.

The writer and speaker Alex Rovira makes a distinction between two kinds of happiness: happiness with a cause and happiness without a cause. The first kind depends on external events and is therefore fleeting:

when our team wins a match, when we win the lottery, when we get promoted. Happiness without a cause comes from inside, for no particular reason, like a transmission from the soul that we can decide to tune in to. We'll work on this unconditional emotion, which puts us in a state of contentment, in the practical section of this book.

Of the four basic emotions we have examined, only happiness belongs to the present and is the home of *ichigo ichie*. Precisely because we know that it is happening only now, and not before or after, we celebrate it by fully giving ourselves over to savoring the moment.

EMOTION	TIME	KEY PHRASE
Anger	Past	Come back!
Sadness	Past	Wake up!
Fear	Future	Come back!
Happiness	Present	*Ichigo ichie!*

Translating Emotions into Time

Since the popularization of the concept of emotional intelligence, we have become increasingly conscious of our feelings, but we are often unaware of how our emotions cause us to travel into the past or the future, and not for pleasure.

In this sense, an exercise as simple as translating emotions into time is a powerful tool for returning to the present, where the happiness, serenity, and attention that characterize *ichigo ichie* can be found.

To achieve this, every time you feel unhappy, you just have to begin to translate it, like this:

- Are you angry/sad? You're living in the past.
  Come back!/Wake up!
- Are you afraid? You're living in the future.
  Come back!

When we stop projecting ourselves into the past or the future, we can recover the happiness of the present.

If we translate emotions into time, it will be much easier for us to escape them, because no one likes being exiled from the present, where important things are happening.

That's why if we realize that we're in the past, we leave. And if we're in the future, we come back.

How Present Are You?

We designed this little quiz to help you evaluate your ability to be in the present and therefore to enjoy the moment.

1. **When I receive a hurtful email, text message, or phone call . . .**
   a) I feel upset and reply right away, but then I forget about it.
   b) I think it over for a while, until I've figured out the right way to respond.
   c) Whether or not I reply, the situation affects me all day—or for several days.

2. I've noticed that a close friend no longer gives me the same attention or affection as before. For my part . . .

a) I don't think it matters much. I figure they must be stressed or have other things going on. We'll see each other again soon, when the time is right.

b) I write a long email and demand to meet up, so I can find out if I did something wrong or if they have some kind of problem.

c) I'm really offended by their neglect and remove them from my list of priorities. If they can't return my affection, then they don't deserve it.

3. I'm going on vacation, and as soon as I arrive at my destination, I find out that the airline has lost my suitcase. Twenty-four hours later, it still hasn't shown up, and . . .

a) I don't let it ruin my trip. I go buy some clothes and the necessary personal items and get on with my vacation. If the suitcase doesn't show up, I'll claim the value of what I've lost when I get home.

b) I proceed with my vacation but I call the airline a couple times a day so they won't stop looking for my suitcase. I continually put pressure on them.

c) I get so upset about not having my clothes and my other things that I have a hard time enjoying my vacation. I can't stop cursing the airline and their useless employees.

4. I read in the paper that the company or sector I work in will soon be hit by a downturn. My reaction is . . .

a) I keep doing my job as best I can, since that's the part I can control.

b) I start calling colleagues who work in the same field to see if the situation is as worrying as I've heard.

c) I feel anxious and start looking for alternatives, in case everything really does go under.

5. I hear that a very enthusiastic teacher whom I really appreciated has a terminal illness.

a) I immediately find out which hospital she's in, so I can go spend some time with her.

b) I start thinking about the fleeting nature of life, and how all good things come to an end.

c) My hypochondria goes into overdrive, and I tell myself that from now on, I should get more regular checkups.

***

Results

(a) is worth zero points, (b) is worth one point, and (c) is worth two points. Calculate your total to see how you did.

Between six and ten points (POOR): You project yourself easily into the past or the future as a result of stress and anxiety that prevent you from enjoying life. You need to learn to come back to the present.

Between three and five points (ROOM FOR IM-PROVEMENT): Your level of nervousness isn't a cause for concern, but if you spent less time brooding over things, your serenity could increase, and you'd no doubt be happier. With a little training, you'll be able to manage it.

Two points or less (GREAT!): Even though events might take you into the past or the future, you know how to return straightaway to the present. You are a master of *ichigo ichie*, with the potential to be an inspiration to others.

The Present Is a Gift to Be Opened

Since the days when the Buddha taught his followers to anchor themselves in the here and now, we have spent 2,500 years in pursuit of that present, which so often melts at our fingertips as if it were snow.

In the next chapter, we'll take a look at some strategies offered by Zen for keeping ourselves in the present, and we'll see how a Japanese monk came to have an influence on Steve Jobs. Before that, though, we'll end this chapter by looking at what happens inside us when we manage to flow in the present, an oasis that insulates us from the suffering of the past and our fears of the future.

A decade ago, in *The Time Paradox*, Stanford psychology professor Philip Zimbardo described the mind that is attentive to the present:

> When you are mindful, you are fully aware of your surroundings and of yourself in the present. Mindfulness increases the time that you swim with your head above water, when you can see both potential dangers and pleasures. When you are mindful, you are aware of your position and your destination. You can make corrections to your path.

For those who spend much of their lives exiled from the present, an experience like this can be transformative. Zimbardo's collaborators Jennifer Aaker and Melanie Rudd demonstrated this in a series of experiments in which they helped several people experience a brief moment of "timelessness."

According to their conclusions, these people "felt they had more time available and were less impatient . . . were more willing to volunteer their time to help other people, [and] more strongly preferred experiences over material products."

As they flowed with the moment, the subjects reported feeling much more satisfied with their lives.

The results of the experiment illustrate why *present* also means gift, and not just in English. The present is always here, and it is offered to us from moment to moment, so that it is unforgettable. However, like any gift, first we must open it.

Next, we will see how to do so.

Zensations

Many things have been said about Steve Jobs, but one relatively unknown aspect of his life is his initiation in Zen, which would be so important to his designs at Apple.

During the two years Jobs spent in college—one and a half of which he attended as an auditor, since he couldn't afford to be fully enrolled—it is said that he spent most of his time reading about religion and Eastern philosophy. He discussed these discoveries with his friend Daniel Kottke, who years later would work on the first Macintosh computers and whose signature was engraved on the inside of those machines.

But before Jobs knew his destiny as an entrepreneur,

when he returned home in 1974, he began to work at Atari, a groundbreaking home video game company, to save money for a trip to Asia.

After a few months, he was able to leave his job and travel to India with Daniel Kottke, who'd caught the spirituality bug from Jobs.

After spending months on end traveling around India by bus, they failed to find a convincing guru. The most interesting event of the trip was when a Hindu monk approached Jobs with a razor and shaved his head without any prior warning.

On his return, Jobs went back to work at Atari for a few months, participating in the creation of the game *Breakout*, until he managed to sell the first Apple Is with his business partner, Steve Wozniak. Just five years later, the company would go public, turning more than three hundred Apple employees into multimillionaires.

ZAZEN SERENITY

Translated literally, zazen (坐禅) means "sitting 坐 zen 禅" and is one of the most popular forms of meditation in Japan. It is traditionally practiced sitting on a cushion, in a lotus or half-lotus position.

The most important thing is to keep your back straight, from your pelvis up to your neck. Your eyes should be directed to the floor, at a distance of about three feet, or watching the wall, as in the case of the zazen meditation of the Rinzai school.

Zazen meditation has no specific goal other than simply centering oneself as much as possible in the present, observing without attachment the things that pass through your mind.

"When you sit still, think about not thinking. How do you think about not thinking? Non-thinking. This is the art of zazen," said Dogen Zenji (1200–1253), considered the founder of this practice.

It is notable that the old master spoke not of making the mind "blank"—often mistakenly considered the goal of meditation—but rather of "not thinking." This means letting go of anything that passes through our mind without becoming attached to it. In this way, we can reach a state without past or future, which allows us to feel every sensation in our body in the present.

The Zazen Years

During this period, Jobs began to practice zazen at the San Francisco Zen Center. There, he met the monk Kobun Chino Otogawa, who would be a friend and mentor for the rest of his life.

It is said that Jobs was one of the students who spent the

most hours meditating. Sometimes, he would take a few days out of his hectic schedule to go to Tassajara, the first Zen monastery in the United States. He would sit in front of a wall and observe his inner state for hours on end. Steve liked the idea of using the mind to study the mind, something known in psychology as "metacognition."

We will learn this technique in the third part of this book, but first let's get to know the guru who left a profound mark on the Apple founder's life.

Born in Kyoto, Kobun Chino Otogawa spent the first thirty years of his life in Japan, three of them in the country's foremost Soto Zen monastery. In the late 1960s, he moved to the United States with the mission of bringing Zen to the West, in addition to teaching haiku and *shodo* calligraphy.

Jobs practiced calligraphy, too. It was important to him that the letters on his computer screens be beautiful. This was just one of the ways he was influenced by his master.

Kobun also taught Jobs the magic of giving one's all to a fleeting moment, the *ichigo ichie* that Kobun had learned in the teahouses.

INSPIRATION FROM
KOBUN CHINO OTOGAWA

"We sit to make life meaningful. . . . We must start simply with accepting ourselves. Sitting brings us back to actually who and where we are."

"The more you sense the rareness and value of your own life, the more you realize that how you use it, how you manifest it, is entirely your responsibility. We face such a big task, so naturally we sit down for a while."

Once, Kobun asked one of his students, "When all the teachers are gone, who will be your teacher?"

The student replied, "Everything!"

Kobun paused, then said, "No, you."

For more than twenty years, until his death in 2002, Kobun Chino Otogawa was a close friend and spiritual mentor to Jobs, at whose wedding he even officiated.

Before founding Apple, Jobs was wondering what to

do with his life, and one of the options that most appealed to him was to dedicate the rest of his life to Zen.

When Kobun Chino Otogawa learned of his plans, he advised Steve against withdrawing from the world, using these words to convince him: "You will find Zen in your everyday life, if you dedicate yourself passionately to what you love. . . . You can still have a spiritual life while you run your business."

In other words, Kobun encouraged Jobs to seek spirituality in his *ikigai*.

Jobs obeyed his master and embarked on an adventure that would revolutionize several industries—computers, phones, and music—forever.

The Japanese Inspiration for Apple

Zen was an essential tool for Jobs when it came to designing his Apple products. One of his guiding principles was to simplify as much as possible, eliminating any element that wasn't strictly necessary.

The iPod, whose simple, beautiful, intuitive design was revolutionary for its time, as well as the iPhone, among other products, demonstrate how much Jobs was influenced by the simplicity he learned from Zen.

However, Jobs didn't travel to Japan for the first time until the early eighties, when he was looking for the most appropriate floppy disk for the first Macintosh. On that trip, he met Aiko Morita, the founder of Sony, and was able to try one of the first prototypes of the Walkman, a device that impressed him. Another thing that fascinated him were the Sony factories, which he used as a model when the time came to build factories for Apple.

While on that first trip to Japan, Jobs took the chance to visit Kyoto and the Eiheiji Soto Zen monastery, where his master had trained before moving to the United States.

Jobs would return to Japan many times throughout his life, and he would always make a stop in Kyoto, his favorite city.

Someone else from Japan whom Jobs admired was the fashion designer Issey Miyake, who focused on seeking elegance through simplicity. Jobs developed quite a personal friendship with him, and it was Issey Miyake who created the legendary turtleneck that Jobs wore almost daily during the later years of his life.

Eight Zen Lessons for an *Ichigo Ichie* Life

Though Steve Jobs was prone to anger, and often treated the people around him unfairly, studying Zen allowed him to bring beauty, simplicity, and harmony to millions of homes with his creations.

The teachings of this Japanese version of Buddhism give us many opportunities to incorporate *ichigo ichie* into our daily lives.

1. *Just sit and see what happens.* Our spiritual shortsightedness often causes us to look far away—in space and time—for what's really right in front of us. Zen teaches us to simply sit and embrace the moment, with no further ambitions than this. If we are with other people, we celebrate their company as a gift.

2. *Savor this moment as if it were your last breath.* You can live only one day at a time, and no one can be certain that they will wake up the next morning. So let's not postpone happiness. The best moment of your life is always this one.

3. *Avoid distractions.* An old proverb says that a hunter who takes aim at two prey at once will kill none. The same thing happens when we try to follow a conversation or read a book at the same time as checking our phone. Zen teaches us to do one thing at a time, as if it were the most important thing in the world. If you do it that way, it undoubtedly will be.

4. *Free yourself from everything that isn't essential.* One can recognize an expert traveler more by what they leave at home than what they carry in their suitcase. Life is a thrilling adventure through which it's best to travel light, so every day, whenever you feel overburdened, ask yourself, What can I let go of?

5. *Be your own friend.* Rather than comparing yourself to others and worrying about what other people think,

assume that you are unique in the world. As the celloist Pau (Pablo) Casals said in a poem written for children: You are a miracle, and there has never been—nor will there ever be—anyone like you.

6. *Celebrate imperfection.* If not even nature in all its complexity, with all its births and deaths, is perfect, then why should you be? Each failure is a sign that you should take a different path. Each flaw is an invitation to polish a diamond. If you have the will to improve, then it's perfect to be imperfect.

7. *Practice compassion.* From a Buddhist perspective, feeling sorry for someone doesn't mean feeling pity but rather a profound empathy that allows us to travel toward the situation of the other to understand their motivations and, if necessary, their mistakes. Each person acts according to the moment of personal growth in which they find themselves. Even when they behave in hateful ways, it's the best they can do with what they have.

8. *Let go of your expectations.* Making predictions, waiting for certain things to happen, is a guaranteed way to kill the

moment. *Ichigo ichie* is experienced with the uncluttered mind taught by Zen.

Regarding this last point, expectations are like the wrapping that prevents us from seeing the gift. Once we have freed ourselves from them, the present offers itself to us in all its splendor.

Dukkha and *Mono No Aware*

The Buddhist concept of *dukkha* is often incorrectly translated as "suffering." A more accurate way of translating it would be: "that slight anxiety and dissatisfaction that all living beings constantly feel inside, because we know that change is inevitable."

Throughout our lives, we often fight to try and escape this feeling rather than accept it. For example, addictions are a form of escapism that we use to calm our *dukkha*.

Contemporary society offers many ways to escape from reality: increasingly immersive video games, internet entertainment, drugs and alcohol, and so forth. Especially when we go through a crisis or suffer a loss, we seek ways to distance ourselves from that sense of impermanence that's so characteristic of our existence.

Nothing lasts forever, neither good nor bad. Accepting this fact is the key to taking full advantage of the sublime moments life bestows on us and to not losing hope when we go through a rough patch.

The Second Arrow

There is a revealing story that tells how the Buddha taught one of his followers a technique for fighting the inevitable *dukkha* that appears in our lives.

"If a person is walking through the forest and is shot by an arrow, is it painful?" asked the master.

"Of course," answered his follower.

"And if he is then shot by a second arrow, is it even more painful?" the Buddha continued.

"Of course, much more than the first."

"The first arrow represents the bad things that happen to us, which we cannot avoid," the Buddha concluded. "Those things over which we have no control. But we are the ones who shoot the second arrow, inflicting unnecessary damage on ourselves."

The second arrow is what, in modern times, has been termed meta-emotion: what we feel about what we have felt.

If something bad happens to us, we will inevitably feel pain, but after the misfortune's initial impact, we tend to react by brooding over what has happened. And when we start mulling it over, feeding the pain of the initial impact, the only thing we achieve is to create more pain. This is the second arrow.

There is no way to protect ourselves from the first arrows, because life is an adventure full of constant risks, but what we can do is avoid shooting ourselves with the second ones, which are the worry and anxiety that arise from thinking about the first.

The Buddha summed it up with perhaps his most famous saying, "Pain is inevitable, suffering is optional."

Some strategies for avoiding the second arrows that poison our existence, far beyond the blows we are dealt by fate:

- *Understand that life is made up of troubles and satisfaction*, and without the former we would be unable to enjoy the latter, since contrast allows us to appreciate the good things in life. Fresh water gives us more pleasure after thirst. Finding love is a far greater privilege after we've experienced being sad and lonely.

- *Be aware of the temporary nature of pain.* The things that wound us don't last forever unless we are determined to lengthen their echo. If we do not wallow in pain, and instead limit ourselves to experiencing it, the pain will gradually fade, and we will be left with a learning experience.

- *Make up for misfortune by enjoying moments of* ichigo ichie. Whether we are alone or in the company of loved ones, the best way to overcome difficulty is by giving ourselves the gift of a beautiful experience that shows us the bright side of life. In the third section of this book, we will see many examples of how to do so.

To summarize, if we accept the first arrow—pain—but don't shoot ourselves with the second—the suffering caused by brooding over our feelings—we can avoid self-punishment and live more lightly, enjoying all of the good things life has to offer us.

Participating in a tea ceremony, playing a sport we like, listening to music, developing a hobby, or approaching time with our friends with a 100 percent *ichigo ichie* attitude reconnects us to life, no matter how much adversity and disappointment we may have experienced.

Mono No Aware

The Japanese expression *mono no aware* is used to express the appreciation of beauty and translates literally as "being aware of the passage of time." We might describe *mono no aware* as "bittersweet," in reference to the strong emotion that overcomes us when we truly realize that the nature of what we are seeing, smelling, hearing, and feeling in the present is ephemeral.

MONO NO AWARE 物の哀れ

哀れ: pathos*

の: of

物: things

The complete expression means: the nostalgia and sadness caused by the impermanence of life and all things that exist.

* In the Aristotelian sense, *pathos* is human feeling that can become existential suffering.

Feeling *mono no aware* is not a negative experience; on the contrary, it means being connected to life's true essence, to the impermanent, and is therefore a direct path to *ichigo ichie*.

The expression *mono no aware* was first used by the eighteenth-century Japanese scholar Motoori Norinaga to describe the general mood of the Japanese people. He was inspired by classic literature, in particular the following two lines from the epic novel *The Tale of the Heike*, written in 1330:

> *The sound of the Gion Shōja bells echoes the impermanence of all things. . . . The proud do not endure, they are like a dream on a spring night.*

Nature provides beautiful moments of *mono no aware*: the blossoming of the *sakura*, the golden light of the setting sun, a light dusting of snow, or a path covered with dry leaves on an autumn day.

These sublime moments deserve our full attention; they charge the batteries of our soul.

Before Motoori Norinaga coined the expression *mono no aware*, the Japanese already had a way of expressing something similar: they would exhale an *"Ahhhhh . . ."* like a kind of sigh.

The history of art and literature is full of these moments of loving what we are about to lose with special intensity—one of the most poignant, poetic feelings that characterize the human condition.

A contemporary example of a novelist who captures the spirit of *mono no aware* is Nobel Prize winner Kazuo Ishiguro, especially in his novels *The Remains of the Day* and *Never Let Me Go*, where characters confront the inevitable passage of time.

Another example is the epic ending of the movie *Blade Runner*:

> *I've seen things you people wouldn't believe. Attack ships on fire off the shoulder of Orion. I watched c-beams glitter in the dark near the Tannhäuser Gate. All those moments will be lost in time, like tears in rain. Time to die.*

The Hedonic Treadmill

This vision of the ephemeral nature of life is also found in the ancient Western world, although it has a different starting point.

In Greece in the third century AD, the stoic philosophers were already practicing negative visualization, which consisted of meditating on the loss of the things you loved. What would happen if your job, your loved ones, and your home were snatched away?

The point of this question was not to cause sadness but to appreciate the preciousness of what one had.

The Romans, who adopted the same philosophy, called this exercise *premeditation malorum*—"the premeditation of evils"—and used it as a tool for giving value to what one had, since when we grow used to something, we often lose interest in it.

The Stoics understood intuitively the dangers of what modern psychology describes as the "hedonic treadmill." This is the mechanism by which, once our desire is quenched, we feel unsatisfied again, because we automatically want what lies one step ahead of us.

For example, if we are used to eating at ten-dollar restaurants, eating at a thirty-dollar restaurant will seem like a luxury. But if, as the years go by, our purchasing power increases and we get used to thirty-dollar restaurants, perhaps we'll start complaining about the food or the service there. To feel satisfied, we'll have to start going to fifty- or hundred-dollar restaurants.

Although it doesn't affect people with an ascetic mentality, the hedonic treadmill is the foundation of consumer society. Once we get what we want, after a brief period of satisfaction, we return to our "base level" of happiness.

This is obvious in people who frequently change partners. Once the novelty has passed and they get used to their new girlfriend or boyfriend, they need to feel the adrenaline produced by being with someone different.

This problem was observed by the Buddha, who identified the source of unhappiness in desire. Unless we can understand the mechanism described here, we will always be unsatisfied and unable to enjoy the happiness of the moment, *ichigo ichie*.

The key to achieving this is to stop orienting ourselves toward new desires, and to begin to sense the magic in everything around us. Happiness lies in wanting nothing outside ourselves, and in appreciating what life has to offer us while it lasts.

MEMENTO MORI

The Latin expression *memento mori* means "Remember that you will die," like the phrase spoken by the

Christian monks we mentioned earlier. Its purpose is to make us always aware that we are here temporarily, and that whether we enjoy the journey depends on us.

It's said that in ancient Rome, whenever a victorious general paraded about the city, someone would follow him, every so often repeating *"Memento mori,"* so that the success wouldn't go to his head.

This same reminder in Latin can be found throughout the Baroque and Renaissance periods, on skulls, statues, paintings, and other works of art that appeal to the ephemeral nature of existence and thus to the famous *Carpe diem!* (Seize the day and don't count on tomorrow).

The Friendly Face of *Carpe Diem*

The *carpe diem* philosophy is commonly associated with excess, with spending money as if there were no tomorrow, but this call to live in the moment also points toward the most beautiful and essential things in life.

A philosopher once said that humans are mortals who act as if they are going to live forever, but rather than making us live like gods, this opens the way to the *enemies of the present*:

- Prioritizing the urgent (for other people) over the important (for us).
- Postponing what we most want to do again and again, as if we had unlimited time.
- Thinking that the conditions aren't right to do what we want to do but that in the future they will be.
- Boycotting the present with feelings of resentment, sadness, and worry that prevent us from enjoying it.

In the face of these ills, *carpe diem*, like Buddhism, reminds us of the impermanence of things. Nothing we love will last forever. Thus, every moment could be the last opportunity.

In this sense, *ichigo ichie* becomes the friendly face of *carpe diem*, since instead of emphasizing the fact that

one day we will die, it reminds us that *today we can live.*
And this, as we will see in the third part of this book, is
a cause for celebration.

As the actress and scriptwriter Mae West said, "You
only live once, but if you do it right, once is enough."

Destiny Depends on a Moment

In 1998, the cult German film *Run Lola Run* was released. The protagonist, played by Franka Potente, has twenty minutes to get hold of 100,000 deutsche marks to save the life of her boyfriend, who has left on a train that same amount of money belonging to his gangster boss. From here, we see events develop in three possible ways, marked by minor differences.

In the first, a dog growls at Lola as she runs downstairs. This makes her run faster, which causes a traffic accident for a man who turns out to be her father's colleague, from whom she hopes to get a loan at the bank where he works.

We then see the second possibility, in which the dog's

owner trips Lola, causing her to fall down the stairs. As a result, her pain makes her run more slowly, which completely alters the course of events on her way to the bank.

In the third possibility, Lola jumps over the dog and reaches the street at a slightly different moment, making for a result different from the previous two.

Beyond this game of possibilities, the film's message is not only that every moment is unique but also that it triggers a completely different set of consequences in a sequence known as the butterfly effect, a phenomenon that has been defined as "sensitivity to initial conditions" and which is part of the chaos theory.

The Butterfly Effect

The term *the butterfly effect* is associated with the popular saying, "A butterfly beating its wings in Hong Kong can unleash a storm in New York." In other words, any change, no matter how small, ends up creating completely different circumstances due to a process of amplification.

Since what happens to us affects others, which in turn affects still others, the initial disturbance ends up changing everything. This theory and the image of the butterfly were proposed by meteorologist and mathematician Edward Norton Lorenz, who postulated that if we had two identical worlds, where the only difference was that in one of them a butterfly was flapping its wings, this world would end up being totally different from the one without the butterfly. In the world with the butterfly, the concatenation—at first negligible—of causes and effects can end up triggering a faraway tornado.

Lorenz discovered this effect in 1960, while working with a rudimentary computer system for predicting the weather. To save space, the printer recording the measurements rounded off one of the numbers slightly by three decimal points (one of the numbers recorded appeared as 0.506 instead of 0.506127).

When this three-decimal-point calculation was introduced into the computer, the weather prediction for two months in advance was completely different from what had been obtained with the six-decimal figure.

This was how Lorenz discovered that any deviation, no matter how minor it seems, ends up being crucial.

Beyond predicting the weather, or extreme circumstances like those of Lola and her boyfriend, let's have a look at some examples to help us understand how the butterfly effect plays out in our daily lives:

- Just as someone jumping in the snow can end up causing an avalanche, a lit cigarette butt can cause a wildfire that burns through an entire landscape, changing the lives of its inhabitants.
- If your mother or father hadn't said the right thing at the perfect moment, their relationship probably wouldn't have blossomed, and you wouldn't have been born or be reading this now.
- When it comes to a scholarship or job listing, taking action instead of thinking "I'll never get it" can result in a radically different life.
- The decision of whether to pursue an idea that crosses our mind can make the difference between starting a great business and nothing happening at all.

The conclusion we can draw from the butterfly effect is this: Though we never know the final consequences of our actions and decisions, every moment holds an essential value. This returns us to an *ichigo ichie* whose effects reach into the future: What you do now will have a unique and totally different result from what you might do at another time.

Amor Fati

The Latin expression *amor fati,* meaning "love of fate," describes the belief that everything that happens in life is for a reason, even though it may not seem so at the time.

Steve Jobs said that it was necessary to "connect the dots" in order to understand later on the true meaning of many of life's events. The belief that everything happens for a reason contains an implicit faith in destiny. But chance also intervenes, as we will see later on.

This doesn't mean that we should give ourselves over to the law of attraction and wait for things to happen. We must mold what chance brings us with a positive attitude and good decisions, according to the cards dealt to us by destiny, as Schopenhauer would say.

The philosopher Friedrich Nietzsche, a contemporary of Schopenhauer's, said the following regarding *amor fati*: Learning to see the beauty of things also allows us to make them beautiful.

While *amor fati* means accepting that everything that happens to us, even when it's unpleasant, happens for a reason, it's up to us to give it a positive meaning, with our attitude and with what we decide to do with what destiny hands us from moment to moment.

FORREST GUMP AND ICHIGO ICHIE

When the movie *Forrest Gump* premiered in Japan in 1995, the subtitle was *ichigo ichie*, and "Tom Hanks" was added before *Forrest Gump*. The full title of the film in Japan was therefore *Tom Hanks Is Forrest Gump, Ichigo Ichie*.

The idea was to emphasize that this is a story in which the protagonist wanders around the world having chance encounters but doesn't allow them to be just any encounters. With a vision of *amor fati*, he puts his heart into being fully present in each of those moments—*ichigo ichie*—even though they might seem irrelevant to his life. This is what makes Forrest Gump such an endearing character.

The Mysterious Role of Chance

In 1971, the writer George Cockroft surprised the world with his novel *The Dice Man*, named by the BBC as one of the fifty most influential books of the last fifty years.

Originally presented as an autobiography with the author's name given as that of the protagonist, *The Dice Man* tells the story of the psychiatrist Luke Rhinehart, who describes his boredom with life as follows: "Life is islands of ecstasy in an ocean of ennui, and after the age of thirty land is seldom seen."

Tired of helping his patients make decisions, many of which turn out to be bad, Rhinehart asks himself a provocative question: *What if we put our most important decisions in the hands of chance?*

Willing to experiment with this idea, he hands his choices over to a couple of dice, which will dictate what he should do based on a list of sometimes ridiculous options he writes himself for each important situation.

This approach affects both Rhinehart's treatment of his patients and his own life. He becomes a man of chance who ends up creating a "six-sided religion," with the dice acting as priest. The basic idea of the novel is that when you put your life in the hands of chance, it will protect you, taking you to the places and situations you need to experience.

Interpreted later as humorous, the dice man's radical *amor fati* demonstrates the fear human beings have of losing control. We believe that we can determine the course of our lives, with the responsibility that entails, but the truth is that chance always intervenes, and sometimes an unexpected detour takes us to our true goal without our knowing it.

An Exercise in Chance

Without going to the extreme of Doctor Rhinehart's barbaric acts in the novel, from time to time we can use an element of chance in our lives, to provide us with a little adventure so that our leisure time can go from being predictable to unique and memorable.

If you don't let a little chance into your life, your experiences will always be the same.

To shake off monotony, we can try to practice chance, say once a month, by writing six options—we'll simplify things by using not two dice, but one die—and taking the option that die dictates. Let's look at a couple of examples:

1. In a bookstore, select six books that were previously unknown to you but that caught your attention for one reason or another, and pick the one that the die indicates. According to the law of chance, the book will contain something we need to read—a clue to our life.

2. To choose a restaurant, apply the same method to six places you've never been before. If you want to take the randomness up a notch, once at the restaurant, you could use the die in every section of the menu, first discarding the options you'd never eat. This way you can experience a meal determined completely by chance.

You can apply this method to choosing a movie to watch, a destination for a weekend getaway, or any other leisure activity. Once a month, handing the reins to chance when making decisions that can have no negative effect provides a different way of living an *ichigo ichie* life.

Meaningful Coincidences

In 1992, Paul Auster published *The Red Notebook*, a collection of thirteen true stories of things that had happened to him in which chance played an essential role, in the form of coincidence or synchronicity.

In one of these, the Brooklyn writer recounts how three years earlier he had found a letter in his mailbox addressed to a certain Robert M. Morgan of Seattle. The postal service had returned the letter to its sender, whose name and address were written on the back of the envelope.

Convinced that he'd never written to any such person, Auster opened the envelope, which contained a typed letter in which a supposed Paul Auster showered

Morgan with praise for the ideas he expressed about one of Auster's books in a college course on the contemporary novel.

In *The Red Notebook*, the real Paul Auster describes the letter as written "in a bombastic, pretentious style, riddled with quotations from French philosophers and oozing with a tone of conceit and self-satisfaction. . . . It was a contemptible letter, the kind of letter I would never dream of writing to anyone, and yet it was signed with my name."

What Auster initially assumed to be a coincidence soon acquired an even more mysterious dimension. A letter ostensibly written by Auster to Morgan had apparently been returned to Auster after reaching the wrong address. The letter's supposed recipient and the writer impersonating Auster were one and the same.

How could the author of this hoax have known Auster's address? What was his motive in letting Auster know that he had usurped his identity?

The author of the *New York Trilogy* never resolved this mystery, but in his book on coincidences, he admits that he has never been able to discard the letter, which still gives him chills every time he sees it. Even so, the author makes sure to keep it on his desk like just another object: "Perhaps it is a way to remind myself that I know nothing, that the world I live in will go on escaping me forever."

Synchronicity: The Message of the Moment

Carl Jung coined the term *synchronicity*, among many other concepts, to refer to the coincidence of two or three events that have no cause-effect relationship even though they have a clear relationship to one another.

As if chance sometimes played with us to turn our attention to things we normally wouldn't notice, here are some everyday examples of synchronicity:

- When a tune comes into your head and suddenly the person sitting in front of you starts humming it.
- When you think about someone you hadn't remembered in a while, and they call you on the phone just at that moment.

It's impossible not to make a connection between these things brought together spontaneously by chance, as if they're trying to attract our attention.

According to Jung, synchronicities can serve the purpose of showing us the importance of a person or a detail that we wouldn't normally notice. He provides this example from his own clinical experience:

A young woman I was treating had, at a critical moment, a dream in which she was given a golden scarab. While she was telling me this dream, I sat with my back to the closed window. Suddenly I heard a noise behind me, like a gentle tapping. I turned round and saw a flying insect knocking against the window-pane from the outside. I opened the window and caught the creature in the air as it flew in. It was the nearest analogy to a golden scarab one finds in our latitudes, a *Scarabaeid* beetle, the common rose-chafer (*Cetonia aurata*), which, contrary to its usual habits, had evidently felt the urge to get into a dark room at this particular moment.

The message this synchronicity provided Jung was that this dream was important for the patient's treatment and must therefore contain clues that were worth interpreting.

A Tool for Conscious Magic

Some people experience many meaningful coincidences while others seem immune to them. Why?

This depends essentially on attention. When we discover coincidences, we become more sensitive to and observant of them, and this helps us begin to detect more.

These subtle messages sent to us by chance are a tool for conscious magic that we can develop in various ways:

- *Paying more attention to what happens around us*: Meetings with others, conversations, books, movies . . . synchronicity is often hidden in everyday details, meaning that it requires a curious and observant outlook.

- *Keeping a diary.* Writing down our day-to-day experiences makes us more aware of the nuances of reality and trains us to pick up on the subtle messages of chance. In psychiatrist Stanislav Grof's opinion, if we notice an instance of synchronicity, we can interpret it as if it were a dream.

- *Talking to creative people.* Jung claimed that synchronicities appear more frequently in the lives of people experiencing a moment of growth or a high degree of creativity. Spending time with these people will help us fine-tune our antenna, since they can show us things we might not otherwise have noticed.

- *Practicing meditation.* This might help us to recognize coincidences more easily, since it anchors us in the moment, where coincidences appear, and it increases the bandwidth of our perception.

Jung pointed out that moments of crisis and transformation are fertile ground for synchronicity, since at these times we are more attentive to signs sent by destiny. In this sense, when we experience many of these special moments, it's as if life is letting us know we're on the right path.

Part II

Living
Ichigo Ichie

The Ceremony of Attention

The Japanese tea ceremony, often called *chanoyu*—literally, the "way of tea"—is much more than a sophisticated ritual for drinking a revitalizing infusion.

It is a ceremony that cultivates the five senses (which we will address in the next five chapters of this section of the book) in the following way:

- *Taste.* The tea served is of the highest quality. Typically, a single cup of extremely pure tea is drunk, and its flavor endures for a long time afterward.
- *Smell.* The scent of the infusion, intense and fragrant, is also important, as are those of the sweets eaten as part of the ceremony. If the ceremony is

conducted in a traditional teahouse, the smells of the wood, the garden's moist soil, and the trees are also part of the experience.

- *Sight.* The tea sets are especially beautiful in their simplicity and are admired and praised as part of the traditional ceremony. The gentle movements of the tea master are also a feast for the eyes, since they perform a precise choreography throughout the ritual.

- *Touch.* Holding the hot cup in your hands before raising it to your lips activates this fourth sense and symbolizes contact with the serenity of the home through *chanoyu.*

- *Sound.* There may be the rustle of the leaves if we are surrounded by trees, and in the modern tea ceremony, participants speak and listen with the utmost attention, according to an etiquette we will explore later on.

Chanoyu is a call for us to pay attention to all five senses and to be anchored in the present, making the ceremony an art that goes far beyond drinking tea.

Now that we know how to make time stop, let's spend a few pages traveling into the past to see how this delicate art came into being.

Raku and *Kintsugi*

In the sixteenth century, the tea master Sen no Rikyū revolutionized the design of the tea ceremony room, reducing it to just two tatami mats, and he was also a great connoisseur of the ritual's different utensils, which in those days were almost always imported from China.

Drawing on his knowledge, Rikyū decided to create a new kind of teacup, called a *raku*. With the help of his friend Tanaka Chōjirō, he designed one that was even more straightforward than the Chinese ones, whose beauty lay in their simplicity.

Rikyū's tearoom and the creation of the *raku* style laid the foundations of what we now consider the Japanese aesthetic.

We can trace back to the same period another key concept of this aesthetic, with profound significance for the human soul: *kintsugi*. Also known as *kintsukuroi*, *kintsugi* is the Japanese art of repairing ceramics with a mixture of lacquer and powdered gold.

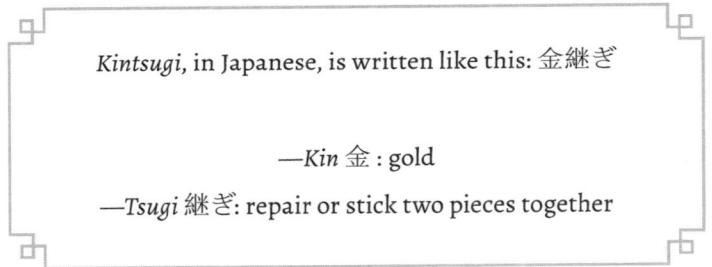

Kintsugi, in Japanese, is written like this: 金継ぎ

—*Kin* 金 : gold
—*Tsugi* 継ぎ: repair or stick two pieces together

The art of repairing broken ceramics was already known in China and can be seen in Zhang Yimou's bucolic film *The Road Home*, a love story about a simple country girl and a schoolteacher, an educated young man from the city.

The young woman has no other way of demonstrating her love than through her cooking, and the bowl in which she prepares food for the teacher ends up getting broken on the road. She is distraught by the loss of a bowl with such emotional value but finds a solution in the form of a roving craftsman who practices an ancestral technique that has almost passed into oblivion. By making precise holes in the ceramic, and with the help of some metal staples, he manages to repair the bowl that symbolizes the young woman's love.

Japanese culture has always distinguished itself by reworking Chinese traditions—sometimes with more sophistication—and this case is no exception.

Legend has it that over five centuries ago, the shogun Ashikaga Yoshimasa sent to China two teacups that had great value for him and had been broken. The cups were returned to him stuck together with staples—the same method used by the craftsman in the film—and at first he was displeased with their crude appearance.

In time, Yoshimasa realized that the bowl repaired in China had a different personality from the rest of his collection. Even though he still didn't like the way it looked, he thought it had character, so he asked some Japanese craftsmen to fill its cracks with the noblest possible material.

That is how *kintsugi* was born. Ceramics are repaired with gold, and the gold lines between the cracks give the ceramics a new aesthetic.

The story goes that Yoshimasa fell so in love with this aesthetic that he asked his artists to deliberately break other pieces of pottery, some of them highly valuable, so that they could be repaired in the same way.

The *Kintsugi* Philosophy

Kintsugi is a radical example of *wabi-sabi*, which teaches us that there is beauty in imperfection. It can also be seen as a metaphor for life, in which we accumulate wounds and losses.

Leaving our emotional wounds exposed forever, like a broken cup that goes unrepaired, causes unnecessary suffering. But we can recover, using what we have learned from our misfortunes and failures. In this way, our scars will tell our stories like the golden lacquer of *kintsugi*.

Just like a delicate piece of porcelain, the human heart can be damaged, but concealing the damage out of shame isn't the solution. The damage is part of our history and has brought us to where we are. Just for this, it deserves the brilliance of gold, which reflects a light that in this case is our own.

PHIL LIBIN'S TREASURE

Phil Libin is the cofounder of tech startups Evernote and All Turtles. He is not only a great Silicon Valley innovator but also a con-  noisseur of all things Japanese who spends a lot of time in Tokyo, where he is a familiar face at technology conferences.

Libin is also a huge fan of *Star Wars*, and he had used the same *The Empire Strikes Back* mug in his office since founding Evernote.

But one day, he dropped it, and it broke into more than ten pieces.

"I swept up the pieces into a plastic bag but was too sad/lazy to throw them out," Libin admits.

When he learned that his mug could be brought back to life through *kintsugi*, he took the pieces to an artist named Shunsuke Inoue, who lives in Fukushima and who managed to repair the mug.

> Libin insists that he likes it even better than the original mug. In his own words, "With the new cracks highlighted in gold lacquer, it's not just restored, it is elevated."

In the purest version of *wabi-sabi*, *kintsugi* doesn't attempt to hide any flaws. Quite the opposite: It highlights them, giving objects a new personality.

Having problems is part of being alive. It is our difficulties and how we face them, more than our periods of contentment, that shape us throughout the course of our lives.

The Cracked Pots

There is an old Indian parable about the beauty and utility of cracks. Thanks to them, we allow the freshest and most creative aspects of ourselves to show through.

The story's protagonist is an Indian water bearer who had two large pots that hung at each end of a pole he carried on his shoulders. One pot was perfect and could retain all the water as the water bearer carried it along the path from the stream to his master's house. The other pot had several cracks and when it arrived at its destination, only half the water remained.

For several years, each pot took its path, and the result was always unequal. The one that knew itself to be perfect was proud of its achievements, impeccably serving the purpose for which it had been created. The cracked pot felt ashamed of its cracks, since it could fulfill only half of its obligation.

On one occasion, its sadness was so great, the cracked vessel decided to speak to the water bearer: "I'm ashamed of myself. I want to apologize to you. Because of my cracks, you can deliver only half my load and are paid only half the money you would otherwise receive."

The water bearer answered, full of compassion: "On the way back, I want you to look at the beautiful flowers growing by the side of the path."

Indeed, the pot noticed that there were many beautiful flowers all along the path. Despite this, it still felt sad, because in the end only half the water arrived at its destination.

"Have you noticed that the flowers grow only on your

side of the road?" the water bearer pointed out. "I've always known you were cracked, and I found the bright side: I planted seeds all along the route we take, and you have watered them each day without noticing. As a result, now I have all these flowers. If you weren't the way you are, with all your cracks, I would still be walking through a desert."

Wabi-cha

Returning to Sen no Rikyū, we're going to tell the story of the originator of the word *wabi* and the *wabi-cha* tea ceremony, along with Takeno Jōō and Murata Jukō.

As we said earlier, it was one of Sen no Rikyū's disciples who was the first to mention the words *ichigo ichie* in his personal notes. Getting to know the essence of *wabi-cha* will help us to better understand why *ichigo ichie* originated in the practice of this discipline.

During Japan's Muromachi period (1336 to 1573), the tea ceremony spread throughout the country, and it featured ornate utensils imported from China. *Wabi-cha* emerged as a reaction to this aesthetic, using utensils with far simpler designs, handcrafted in Japan.

In addition to these minimalist utensils, *wabi-cha* is also known for having simplified the place where the tea ceremony was performed.

The rooms designed by Sen no Rikyū were just large enough for two people. One of the tearooms originally designed by this great master still exists today. Designated a national treasure, it is called Taian, and is located to the south of Kyoto, near the Yamazaki station. The structure of the Taian room has been used as a model for other rooms where *wabi-cha* is practiced.

- The room consists of only two tatami mats, with a small area in the corner to heat water for the tea. Until then, the smallest rooms had had four and a half tatamis.
- There is also a *tokonoma*, a nook at the end of the room where there is a hanging scroll bearing a poetic message, perhaps the motto *ichigo ichie*. In fact, it is found in all kinds of tearooms.

- A corner of the room is reserved for the cast-iron kettle, which is made using a sand mold or, in modern times, a furnace.

Illustration of a tearoom designed according to the standards established by Sen no Rikyū. There is very little space, with one tatami for each person: the guest and the tea master.

The minimalist *wabi-cha* space creates a unique sensory world where it is difficult to escape into the past or future. It forces us to focus on the present, since the only other things in the room are the other person, two tatamis, the tea, and a scroll bearing a message.

Sen no Rikyū designed the room this way so that the practice of *wabi-cha* would be as direct and honest as possible, without any form of distraction. This mythical tea master also believed that *wabi-cha* provided a way of getting to know oneself in the most honest way possible.

ECONOMY OF COLOR

In Japan, when one color takes center stage, an effort is made to prevent the interference of others. For example, in wooded areas, where greens and ochers are dominant, Buddhist temples blend in like chameleons, using wood and other natural tones, so as not to stand out against the forest but instead to form part of it.

As an exception, inside the main building of a Buddhist temple, other shades, like gold, are allowed, to give the impression of having entered a different space or world.

Economy of color is present in the rooms with tatamis where the tea ceremony is performed. The walls are of similar shades to the tatamis. The idea is that the attention of those present should not be absorbed by a mix of colors.

When the tea is ready, green stands out above all else.

Create Your Own Tea Ceremony

Given our connection to Japan, we have had the opportunity to enjoy the *chanoyu* in many teahouses. After the adventure in Kyoto with which this book began, we said goodbye to each other in Tokyo, in a modern Ippodo chain teahouse, where silence and harmony prevailed.

A server delicately brought us a tray with our chosen tea, which we could see—and smell—in a small vessel we would use to brew ourselves, along with a kettle, a cup, and a sweet.

Without a tea master to perform the ritual, we took charge of making that *chanoyu* memorable, and before going our separate ways at the door of the Narita Express—the high-speed train that links the capital to the international airport—we gave each other a hug and wished each other goodbye, saying *ichigo ichie.*

Times have changed, and nothing is forcing us to carry out strict tea ceremonies like Sen no Rikyū's, though if you're visiting Japan for the first time, it's a beautiful experience to have once in your life.

In our day-to-day lives, though, *chanoyu* can be carried out anywhere: in a public teahouse, with the participants seated around a table; or just in a living room, in the company of friends. The important thing is that when the tea is served, you allow time to be still, putting daily worries, criticisms, and complaints out of your mind.

It's essential for those participating in the ceremony to do so with their hearts full of *ichigo ichie.* In other words, they should appreciate that the time they will spend drinking tea with the rest of those present is something extraordinary that will never happen again.

A few rules of etiquette for our version of *chanoyu:*

- The meeting place should inspire calm. Meeting in bars or restaurants with loud music, or spaces not insulated from the sound of traffic, is not recommended.

- Begin the meeting with the greeting *ichigo ichie*, to remind yourselves that you are going to experience a moment that won't be repeated.

- As the ceremony unfolds, allow space for silence and don't insist on "filling the void" with just any old conversation.

- When you speak, avoid any potentially controversial, unpleasant, or stressful topics. Any issue that sows division should be off-limits.

- Instead, encourage topics of conversation that make the participants feel at ease: comments on the uniqueness of the place, the quality of the tea, and the beauty of the teapot; your recent artistic or cultural discoveries; recommendations of travel destinations, restaurants, or parks . . . basically anything that's pleasant to talk about.

- Listening is essential to making everyone feel part of the ceremony. For this reason, you should avoid interrupting others or getting distracted from what they are saying by thinking about your own concerns or rehearsing your answers.

- At the end of the *chanoyu*, say goodbye with *ichigo ichie*, to remind yourselves that you have experienced something unique that will never happen again in the same way and that is therefore a memory deserving to be treasured.

HAVING TEA WITH YOURSELF

Although the *chanoyu* ceremony was conceived for at least two people—traditionally the tea master and a guest—it's a great idea to have a regular "tea with yourself," as the Uruguayan author Walter Dresel suggested.

Constantly tied up with commitments and external obligations as we are, a date with ourselves once a week can be a true balm for the soul.

You can set aside a fixed time and day every week to spend in a café or teahouse that you find inspiring. Once you have ordered your tea, give yourself the gift of that time to think, take notes in a journal, or simply breathe deeply and take in the world around you with all five of your senses.

The Art of Listening

It's difficult to find someone who truly listens, since between someone else's words and our ears, there are all kinds of filters and obstacles. Some of these are:

- Our opinion of the person speaking.
- All of our prejudices and preconceived ideas about the topic.
- Our thoughts about what we're going to say when the other has finished speaking.

All of this makes us listen only superficially, even when we don't directly interrupt the person we're talking to.

To experience moments of *ichigo ichie* in the company of others, it's essential to practice the art of listening, a gift given to us by nature even in the months leading up to our birth.

Listening before Birth

Babies can hear even before they're born. In fact, half-way through a pregnancy, a fetus can already follow its mother's heartbeat and other sounds made by her body. From within the uterus, it hears the sounds of digestion and everything that happens inside its first home.

From the sixth month on, it can hear even what happens outside the mother's body. It's no fantasy on the part of parents who say that their babies react excitedly to their words by moving and kicking in the womb.

It has also been shown that we are sensitive to music before birth, as well as to any other sound made in the home.

This innate attention continues to develop after we are born, but as we grow up, inner and outer distractions begin to undermine our ability to perceive clearly what happens around us.

CONNECTED OR SEPARATE

"We spend most of our moments when someone is speaking, planning what we're going to say, evaluating it, trying to come up with our presentation of our self, or controlling the situation. Pure listening is a letting go of control. It's not easy and takes training.

The bottom line is when we are listened to, we feel connected. When we're not listened to, we feel separate."

—Tara Brach, *The Sacred Art of Listening*

Noise Pollution

In our personalized tea ceremony, we emphasized the importance of the participants gathering in a quiet place, without background music, because there is a direct relationship between noise and our capacity for attention, which is diminished by stress.

It's estimated that if someone talks while we're trying to read or write, our productivity is reduced by 66 percent.

At the opposite extreme, an experiment conducted on the London Underground showed that pleasant sounds reduced crime. The Underground authorities decided to play classical music at a station with a high incidence of theft and assault. Much to the surprise of the initiative's promoters, cases of theft dropped by 33 percent, while attacks on Underground staff dropped by 25 percent, according to a report published in *The Independent.*

It's also interesting to see how groups that don't suffer from noise pollution develop extraordinary hearing abilities. This is why communities living in the jungle or in rural areas, as well as monks and nuns, are the groups that listen best.

Some Keys to Being a Better Listener

Whether we are practicing *chanoyu* or some other celebration, or just want to get along better with our partner, family members, friends, or coworkers, these simple steps can improve the quality of our listening, as well as that of others:

- *Find the right place for important conversations.* An office with loud voices and ringing phones isn't the best atmosphere for quality communication, and neither is a living room with a television or music at full volume. The first step toward good listening is to do all you can to avoid any source of noise pollution.

- *Look your interlocutor in the eye.* With direct eye contact, we can let our interlocutor know that they matter to us and that we are completely present. However, this eye contact shouldn't be intimidating. We should pay attention to the other person's verbal language and make sure they feel comfortable with the amount of physical space between us. This information is valuable and will allow us to make adjustments.

- *Turn off interfering thoughts.* As we mentioned at the beginning of this chapter, we all have a natural tendency to place filters between ourselves and those we speak to. The key is not to judge. If we limit ourselves to listening to what someone else has to say, we'll be able to absorb their whole message, and the person will feel heard. For this to happen, we need to prevent our mind from wandering and maintain the discipline of being present.

- *Ask questions without interrupting.* It's important not to cut people off, since this can cause frustration. What they *will* value is being asked questions that demonstrate we are still listening. These can be to find out more about what they're telling us or just to let them know we haven't lost track of what they're saying. To do so, we can interject by saying things like, "So you're saying that . . ." This kind of active listening will be a true gift to those we speak to.

- *Don't give unsolicited advice.* When someone shares a problem, it can be difficult not to offer a solution, but often what the other person needs most is to be listened to, not to be told what to do. If we think we have something valuable to offer regarding their situation, we can ask, "Can I give you some advice?" or offer a solution indirectly: "Of course, only you can know the right thing to do, but if I were in your position, I would . . ."

If we approach our conversations respectfully, giving them our full attention, the possibility will increase that each encounter, in addition to deepening our connections, will end up being unforgettable.

The Art of Looking

Sight is the most highly developed human sense, though unfortunately we spend more time watching life go by on-screen than looking at it directly.

Much as it might entertain us, it's impossible to experience anything memorable while surfing the web or plugged into social media, precisely because of the instant, throwaway nature of these interfaces. Whatever appears on-screen now that we might share with others will be forgotten in twenty-four hours, if not sooner.

In order to have *ichigo ichie* experiences, we need to regain our ability to *look life in the eye.*

Looking and Seeing

Ninety percent of the information that reaches our brain is visual, but that doesn't mean we know how to use our eyes, which are so essential for most people. Many people *look without seeing*. In other words, they don't pay attention to what's in front of them.

There is a story about Ronald Reagan attending a university award ceremony when he was still in good health. The president of the United States was known for his considerable social intelligence. Wherever he went, he knew how to connect with the group and had people eating out of his hand with his charm.

At this award ceremony, though, he failed to recognize his own son, who was there to receive a prize and was standing barely a few feet away. He was so focused on his role in the spotlight that for a few seconds he didn't see who was right in front of him.

This is a case of looking without seeing, something that happens often in our daily lives, and not just when we bump into other pedestrians on the street while absorbed in our cell phones.

Gymnastics for the Eyes

We're not talking about a blind person recovering their sight, but on a metaphorical level it's equally significant. The purpose of the exercises we suggest here is to fine-tune this precious tool, to capture the beauty of the world through our eyes.

- It's easy to feel overstimulated in cities, and not just by the noise pollution. Try to get out into the countryside once a week to regain your ability to see. Forests make for a fascinating visual experience. As well as paying attention to different species of trees and plants and to the birds and insects that give life to the landscape, noticing phenomena like *komorebi*—the play of sunbeams filtering through tree branches, an example of the abstract art in nature—helps us enrich and enhance our sight.

- When you walk to work, or go out to run errands, instead of becoming a zombie absorbed in your smartphone, pay attention to the details of your city that usually pass you by. Notice the buildings, the color of the sky, and the shapes of the clouds floating by. In other words, use your eyes to appreciate the world around you, as if you were in an enormous gallery.

- When you meet up with other people, pay attention not only to the meeting place but also to the details and nuances that reveal your friends' emotional state and intentions. Do they look relaxed, or maybe they're sitting up straight and look tense? What are they doing with their hands? Is their gaze steady, or are they distracted? This kind of attention will give us a deeper look, both literally and metaphorically, at who each person is and at how they are, right here and right now.

HOW TO LOOK AT A PAINTING

Wassily Kandinsky, a major artist of the twentieth century avant-garde, gave the following advice for viewing art: "Lend your ears to music, open your eyes to painting, and . . . stop thinking! Just ask yourself whether the work has enabled you to 'walk about' into a hitherto unknown world. If the answer is yes, what more do you want?"

Art museums are wonderful places to learn the art of looking. Here are a few keys to an *ichigo ichie* experience within the walls of an art gallery:

- One mistake often made in a museum is wanting to "see it all," since most of us have a limited attention span. After fifty or sixty works, or maybe fewer, it's easy to feel tired and overwhelmed. To avoid this, it's best to choose just one part of the collection, or even the works of a particular artist who interests us.
- During your visit, choose three to five paintings that stood out for you. If there's a place to sit in front of a painting, as is often the case with important works, even better.
- Take at least five minutes to look at each of these paintings. Once you've seen a painting as a whole, focus on the details, allowing yourself to be absorbed in the canvas, as if you were part of it.

- Then, ask yourself questions like these: What story is this painting trying to tell? What might have inspired the painter? What kind of feelings does the painting inspire? Is there anything here that I can connect to my life? If it happens to be an abstract painting, focus on the last two questions.

- Before leaving the museum, if you can buy postcards of these paintings in the museum store, you can use them later as a reminder of the *ichigo ichie* moment you had looking at them.

The Art of Touching

The poet Paul Valéry said that "the deepest thing in man is the skin." Sometimes, our most emotionally powerful feelings come from being touched. How can we forget the first time we held hands with someone we felt attracted to? Not to mention our first kiss . . .

There are moments of *ichigo ichie* that culminate in touch, which we often don't pay enough attention to and which is also an essential human need.

Research by the American Psychiatric Association found that a simple hug has the power to reduce levels of cortisol, the stress hormone that, if secreted continuously, can have devastating effects on our health. Another study, at the University of Miami in 2010, showed that when we hug someone, our skin's receptors send a message to the nerve in our brain responsible for reducing blood pressure.

Touching and hugging are beneficial even as a preventive therapy for many life-threatening illnesses.

Four hugs a day are considered enough to boost a person's emotional and physical health, but according to international relations expert Andy Stalman, the ideal number is eight six-second hugs a day. Six seconds is apparently the minimum length of time required for oxytocin—the hormone associated with happiness—to reach the brain, awakening feelings of trust and affection.

THE BENEFITS OF TOUCH

As well as giving us moments to remember, regular physical contact offers the following benefits:

1. *It lowers blood pressure and facilitates general relaxation,* decreasing headaches and improving sleep quality. This explains why we usually sleep better after sexual intercourse.

2. *It communicates a sense of trust and intimacy* that can't be obtained through words alone. A conflict that many arguments have failed to resolve can dissipate after a long, sincere hug.

3. *It motivates us to be successful.* Dacher Keltner, the author of *Born to Be Good: The Science of a Meaningful Life*, tells us that members of sports teams who congratulate each other with hugs or high fives achieve better results than those who don't interact physically.

4. *It strengthens relationships.* Sexologists point out that couples who engage in frequent physical contact have a higher level of empathy and stay together longer than those for whom physical contact is purely sexual.

5. *It lifts your mood.* A big hug or even a relaxing massage can help dissipate negative feelings that have built up during a bad day.

Boris Cyrulnik's Discovery

For half a century, Boris Cyrulnik, a French neurologist and psychiatrist who experienced the horrors of Nazi concentration camps, has been studying the importance of affection to human equilibrium.

After the fall of the Romanian dictator Ceaușescu, Doctor Cyrulnik worked with children in Romanian orphanages who for the first ten months of their lives had experienced no physical affection. A neurological study of these children revealed that they were suffering from atrophy in the prefrontal cortex and the amygdala.

According to Cyrulnik, author of *The Ugly Ducklings*, among other books, this was the result of the lack of sensory stimulation they received from their caretakers, who had limited themselves to providing food and essential medical attention.

Among the children who had reached the age of five, 10 percent showed signs of serious psychological disturbance, and 90 percent showed behavior similar to autism, all of which was a consequence of that lack of affection.

In view of this situation, the children were sent to

foster families who provided them with great care and attention. And then, the miracle happened: After just a year, almost all the children recovered, and their prefrontal cortices were able to develop again.

Activities to Awaken Touch

If we want to include all five senses in our unique moments, it's worth regularly exercising our sometimes-neglected sense of touch. A few ideas:

- When you touch something with your hands, like a gnarled tree trunk, close your eyes and imagine that you have ears and eyes in your hands.
- Make a habit of touching things in your day-to-day life. When buying an item of clothing, before trying it on, touch the fabric to feel its texture.
- When you step out onto the street, be aware of the weather against your skin: feel the cold or the warmth of the sun, the humidity, the breeze . . .
- Try walking barefoot on surfaces that can't harm your feet, such as wood, grass, or even dirt, to

awaken the sensitivity in the soles of your feet. Feel how they support the weight of your body and how they move to balance it.

The chess champion Bobby Fischer, considered a highly cerebral person, once said that "nothing is so healing as the human touch," but this sense shouldn't be limited to serving as a comfort. We can be like children holding hands in a circle and let touch be part of our celebration of life.

The Art of Tasting

With the rise in popularity of global cuisine, our sense of taste is increasingly alert. But we can still give it a larger role in our pursuit of unique experiences.

One of the most surprising of these experiences has been *Dans le noir* restaurants, which offer the unusual and undoubtedly memorable experience of dining in total darkness, with blind waiters providing the service.

Established in Paris in 2004, *Dans le noir* is the world's first restaurant chain of its kind. It offers its diners totally new culinary adventures, such as the following:

- Guessing what they are eating: This isn't always easy, since smells and textures can become confused without the benefit of sight.

- Guessing what they are drinking: Ninety percent of customers are unable to tell the difference between white wine, red wine, and rosé.
- Listening more intently: When dining in the dark, the diners' only awareness of other tables is what they hear, which contributes to the sharpening of this sense, as happens with the blind.

The Universe in an Apple

Inspired by this new restaurant trend, the following exercise seeks to achieve the full attention that the Vietnamese monk Thich Nhat Hanh recommends: "There is nothing else filling your mind as you chew—no projects, no deadlines, no worries, no 'to do' list, no fears, no sorrow, no anger, no past, and no future. There is just the apple."

Unless you don't like apples, in which case you should choose another fruit, you can practice this mindfulness exercise in the following way:

1. Blindfold yourself, making sure you can't see anything.
2. Take an apple in your hand and feel its weight and
   its hardness, and the texture of its skin.
3. Lift the apple to your nose and calmly breathe in
   its scent. This will also allow you to enjoy its flavor
   much more, since taste and smell reinforce each
   other.
4. Take a bite. Before chewing, feel its flesh on your
   tongue. Notice what happens to your saliva, then
   feel it beneath your tongue as well.
5. Chew the piece of apple as if it were the only thing
   in the universe.

MOOD AND FLAVOR

Research conducted in 2015 by Doctors Robin Dando
and Corinna Noel with a group of hockey fans shows
how mood affects our sense of taste.

When the local team won, its fans enjoyed flavors
they hadn't previously liked. But when the team lost,

sweetness lost its potency and bitterness became more unpleasant.

A good mood, helped along by pleasant company, is an essential ingredient for enjoying our food.

Umami: The Fifth Flavor

Our sense of taste used to play an essential role in our survival, since it allows us to get to know the characteristics of foods we may not have tried before.

Sweetness signals a food that could provide energy. A savory taste indicates foods rich in salts essential for the body. Bitterness and acidity are warning signs.

A fifth flavor, especially valued by the Japanese, is *umami*, associated with food with a high level of amino acids.

At the end of the nineteenth century, the origin of the *umami* (旨味: 旨 delicious, 味 flavor, in Japanese) that we taste in fermented foods—like a good cheese, a cured ham that isn't too salty, or a ripe tomato that's neither sweet nor acidic—still hadn't been identified.

This diagram shows the areas of the tongue where different flavors are tasted.

An experiment conducted on Japanese babies, in which the babies' reactions to foods with bitter, acidic, sweet, and *umami* flavors were assessed by observing their facial expressions, demonstrated that in addition to the pleasure produced by sweetness, *umami* generated a serene expression.

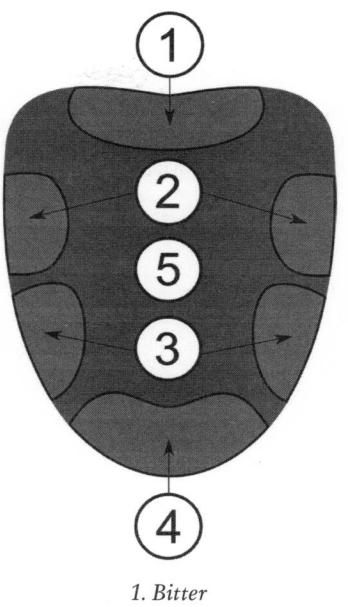

1. *Bitter*
2. *Acidic*
3. *Salty*
4. *Sweet*
5. *Umami*

The Japanese discovered *umami* in *kombu* kelp and *katsuobushi* (bonito flakes), but it is also present in miso soup and in soy sauce.

Another interesting fact about *umami* is that breast milk is high in glutamate, a key amino acid in foods like *kombu*, or edible kelp.

In the United States it can be found in ketchup, for example, but there are many more foods associated with "the fifth flavor" in cuisines all over the world.

When a food tastes neither sweet nor acidic, bitter, or salty but it's delicious . . . it's *umami*!

The Art of Smelling

One fact that demonstrates what little we know about smell is that humans can recognize up to ten thousand different aromas, but most people have few more than ten adjectives to define them.

Another special feature of smell is that it is intimately linked to taste, as we noted in the previous chapter. This is why people who lose their sense of smell also cease to enjoy food, as they can no longer distinguish flavors from one another.

There's something special about our most mysterious sense, since it works with what's invisible and is the sense most closely linked to memory.

It must have happened to you. You walk into a place and you're seized by a familiar scent. It could be a perfume, an air freshener, the smell of the wood, or anything else, but it stops you in your tracks. The familiar fragrance transports you to a different time, perhaps to a concrete situation, to some moment that was dormant in your memory and now suddenly awakens.

In his multivolume novel *In Search of Lost Time*, Marcel Proust described a similar moment of epiphany with a madeleine dipped into a cup of tea: "This new sensation having had on me the effect which love has of filling me with a precious essence; or rather this essence was not in me, it was myself. I had ceased now to feel mediocre, accidental, mortal. Whence could it have come to me, this all-powerful joy?"

The Time Machine

We may not have invented the vehicle described by H. G. Wells in his famous sci-fi novel *The Time Machine*, but we have access to a far simpler and more immediate vehicle: our sense of smell.

More than any other, this sense has the ability to make us travel back in time, recovering *ichigo ichie* moments thanks to the aromas that open the way to the brain's hippocampus and amygdala, associated with learning and emotions.

According to Guillermo Bértolo, account manager at the agency Dejavu Brands, "Human beings memorize three percent of what we see, five percent of what we hear, and thirty-five percent of what we smell."

This is difficult to verify, but it's clear that our sense of smell is the one with the greatest power of evocation. The smell of wet earth after rain, or of chlorine in a swimming pool, can take us very far back in time.

But our nose's subtle power takes us far beyond memory and the appreciation of different fragrances.

A SMELL JOURNAL

To strengthen this subtle antenna in our perception tool kit, it can be useful to keep a journal. Each time an aroma transports you to a specific time and place, write it down in your notebook. With time, you will have a pocket "travel agent"; in order to buy a ticket, you need only breathe in the right aroma, close your eyes, and let yourself be transported.

A Cabinet of Aromas

In the temples of Asia, incense is used to transport visitors to another place. You can reproduce this experience at home with incense or scented candles to summon other places and states of mind.

The art of aromatherapy has been practiced for millennia in countries like China, India, and Egypt, where it was used to prevent and treat illnesses, including those of the soul.

Let's take a look at the properties attributed to three of the most popular essential oils:

- *Pine for stress relief.* In a study conducted at the University of Kyoto, 498 volunteers took two fifteen-minute walks in a pine forest on the same day. At the end of the day, those who had previously been feeling sad, nervous, or angry reported relief. In fact, the most stressed were those who showed the most dramatic improvement. Though we might not have a forest nearby, the scent of pine in an essential oil can provide this sense of peace.

- *Lavender for sleep.* Numerous studies show that this plant with purple flowers is an excellent cure for insomnia, thanks to its tannins, flavonoids, and other natural substances that reduce anxiety and help to ease muscle tension, facilitating rest.
- *Mint for concentration.* Known since ancient times to have an invigorating effect on the mind, mint is used by many college students in the United States to optimize focus while studying. It can also revive the body after an exhausting day, and thus a few drops of mint oil are often used in the bath.

In the Japanese chain Muji, which can be found in many countries, these fragrances can be seen in the form of candles and incense or in essential oils for use in aromatherapy mist diffusers.

Among other scents, we can find unusual ones like burning firewood, which turns out to be surprisingly realistic.

Given the connection between smell and memory, if we want to create better memories for the future in the present, introducing a distinctive aroma will help make an experience memorable.

THE MOON ABOVE THE TOWER

The most well-known Japanese perfume was created by Issey Miyake, the designer Steve Jobs chose to create a personalized version of his famous black turtleneck.

In 1992 he launched L'eau d'Issey. The stylized bottle with its spherical cap was inspired by the view one night, from his Paris apartment, of the full moon above the Eiffel Tower.

Miyake was born in Hiroshima in 1938 and was eight years old when the atomic bomb was dropped, something he has always avoided discussing. Even so, he says that each time he closes his eyes, he sees "things no one should ever experience." The bomb caused his mother's death from radiation three years later.

Miyake's dedication to the world of fashion is connected to this terrible experience: "We yearn for the beautiful, the unknown, and the mysterious. . . . [I prefer] to think of things that can be created, not destroyed, and that bring beauty and joy."

Part III

The Little School of *Ichigo Ichie*

The Art of Parties

The art of creating ceremonies that linger in our hearts isn't exclusive to Eastern cultures. In the West, too, certain people have embodied the true spirit of the tea masters in various realms.

One of these is Étienne de Beaumont. Little known outside France, in the interwar period, this count who was also an arts patron, decorator, fashion designer, and librettist was known for throwing unforgettable parties.

In 1918 in Paris, he organized an enormous jazz concert by recruiting a group of African American soldiers. He hosted balls with themes like "The Sea" or "Famous Paintings." He also staged "Les Soirées de Paris," mixing cabaret, poetry, ballet, and theater with the participation of such artists as Jean Cocteau, Pablo Picasso, and Erik Satie.

The last party he threw was the 1949 "Ball of Kings and Queens," in which Christian Dior appeared dressed as a lion, the king of the jungle.

Étienne de Beaumont undoubtedly knew how to create *ichigo ichie* at his parties—he never repeated the same idea. Those who attended his events knew that each was a unique opportunity. De Beaumont was an expert in *the art of parties*—like the title of the British band Japan's best-known song—and he knew how to make sure that his parties were never remotely predictable.

In fact, it is de Beaumont who is reputed to have said, "Parties are mostly thrown for those who aren't invited."

X-Ray of a Failure

Many people agree that most parties are boring unless there are friends there whom we enjoy talking to.

At a private celebration we were once invited to, there

were tables overflowing with excellent catered food, all kinds of drinks, careful decoration, candles, music.

Next to a loudspeaker we saw a man dancing alone, which made us feel strangely sad. The rest of the guests were sitting on couches and armchairs, looking shy or tired, or even fed up. Most of the guests didn't know one another, and, given that we arrived toward the end of the night, all of the "elevator conversations" seemed to have been used up.

What went wrong? The party seemed to have everything it needed to satisfy the guests: good food and drinks, a comfortable, well-decorated space, soft music, an international atmosphere . . .

But there was an ingredient lacking that Étienne de Beaumont wouldn't have forgotten: a theme to make it a memorable occasion.

Keys to an *Ichigo Ichie* Party

Much like a novel or a movie needs something to tie together its succession of events so it doesn't bore us, a memorable celebration should have something to give it focus.

In order to imbue an event with *ichigo ichie*, the key question we should ask ourselves is this:

What should this party be remembered for?

The answer should be the theme of the gathering. Let's look at a few situations that can give these parties a focal point:

- A concert, given by the host or by a guest musician. This will create anticipation, giving guests something to look forward to.
- A screening of a brief documentary about a specific place or country, accompanied by refreshments inspired by the regional cuisine. This will give focus and meaning to what happens around the table, just like the *chanoyu*.
- A task involving all the guests. For example, an end-of-year gathering at which each guest shares a New Year's resolution with the others providing encouragement to help see it through.

- A shared game that allows people to get to know one another. For example, ask everyone to bring a meaningful object and, at a certain point during the dinner or gathering, give them an opportunity to explain why it's so special to them: what memories or feelings it awakens or its message, if it has one. This will make for a magical evening, allowing people to connect and leaving them with indelible memories.

The key to a successful theme is that it should have the potential to summon an emotional response from the guests.

This requires:

- Understanding the guests (so you can also avoid potentially offensive topics).
- Looking for common ground so everyone feels included.

THE SAVAGE ORACLE

Surrealists like André Breton and his friends in the artistic avant-garde of the early and mid-twentieth century used chance as a way to create new and suggestive meanings at their gatherings. Without their knowing it, they were pursuing *ichigo ichie*.

A perfect game for breaking the ice at an event is one known as The Savage Oracle. It's a simple game, and it goes like this:

1. Each guest is given half of a blank page or a page folded in two.

2. Ask the guests to write a question on one side of the paper—about something they would like to know about themselves. The question should begin with *Why* and should be asked in the first person singular. (For example: "Why am I always in a bad mood when I wake up?")

3. Next, ask the guests to turn over their paper and to let their minds go blank. Then ask them to

write down the first thing that comes into their mind that has nothing to do with the question they wrote down. It should begin with *Because* and be written in the second person singular. (For example: "Because you were born too late.")

4. Now divide the group in two. One group will ask what they want to know about themselves, and the other will respond with the random answer they wrote down.

5. Then change roles so that those who have re-sponded can ask their question and get an answer.

A Permanent Romance

When talking to others about his relationship, a friend of ours likes to say, "I'm the love of her life," and his part-ner will often respond: "But you have to make me fall in love again every day!"

And she is right. The secret to successful long-term relationships is for couples to share many moments of *ichigo ichie*. They don't take anything for granted, and they work on the small, everyday details of their lives to keep the flame burning.

This means escaping the patterns that lead many couples who follow an unvarying script for their lives to boredom: a quick breakfast, work, dinner at home, fall asleep in front of the TV, go to bed.

Day after day, this shared routine is a sure path to apathy, and sometimes to instances of adultery that might not have happened had the couple worked to preserve the chemistry of the beginning of their relationship.

With the spirit of *ichigo ichie* we can take the initiative—at least one day a week—to avoid falling into predictable patterns. A couple of examples:

- Giving a gift—with sentimental value; it doesn't have to cost anything—for no reason.
- Transforming your dining room at home with atmospheric music, candles, and your best china and silverware. You can even put a printed menu on the table.

The most important thing is to make a break from the inertia of the everyday by creating a story, something that deserves to be reminisced about. In fact, when we work consciously on *ichigo ichie*, we are creating our future memories—ones that can strengthen a couple's bonds, thanks to shared experiences.

If we want to be able to look back on our lives with happiness and nostalgia, we can't allow the present to be just a succession of days. We have the magic of our will to turn every encounter into something special.

Ichigo Ichie at Work

Who said a work meeting has to be boring? Why not apply the art of parties to work, which takes up a third of our lives?

To honor this idea, we decided that when we introduced the idea for this book at the London Book Fair, our presentation should embody *ichigo ichie*. Instead of having a typical presentation in a convention center, we organized a special and memorable event for our international publishers:

- We rented a Japanese tearoom in central London, where we invited our publishers to relax after an exhausting day at the fair.
- In the room reserved for our guests, the tearoom staff served three kinds of tea: *genmaicha* (brown rice green tea), *kukicha* (twig tea) with *sakura* blossoms, and a macrobiotic *bancha* (a type of green tea), as well as the right sweets for our particular *chanoyu* ceremony.
- We prepared a short video about *ichigo ichie* in Japan and played it in the tearoom to welcome our guests.
- After giving our publishers an extract from the book, and explaining the book's concepts, we arranged for the tea and cakes to be served, while *BTTB*—our favorite album by the Japanese composer Sakamoto—played in the background.
- This allowed our publishers from around the world to relax and talk among themselves in a purely Japanese atmosphere.

- At the end of the evening, we parted with our guests by saying "*Ichigo ichie*," happy to have shared this unforgettable evening with them.

The art of throwing parties, no matter what kind—whether it's a convention or a dinner for two—is essentially the will to create a unique experience that will enrich the lives of all who attend.

And to achieve this, as the Beatles song goes, all you need, apart from attention and an inspiring ritual, is love. The success of your gathering will be proportionate to the care and time you invest in it, something in which the Japanese—great lovers of detail—are true masters.

Collective Mindfulness

At the beginning of this book we mentioned Yamanoue Sōji, the tea master who in 1558 introduced for the first time the concept we are trying to work into our lives. The meaning of what he said was, "Treat your host with *ichigo ichie*."

What did he mean by this? What does it mean to treat someone as if the encounter were going to happen only once in a lifetime?

Above all, it means paying attention. To what we're doing, to the other person's needs (for example, sensing from them when we should stop talking), and to the magic of a shared moment.

The Source of (Almost) All Conflicts

Many of the problems we experience in our daily lives as individuals—and on a macro scale as a society—have their origin in a lack of attention to others.

In our globalized world we have the chance to connect with thousands, even millions, of people, but it's extremely rare to find someone who really knows how to listen. And listening is an essential gift, as we have seen in the chapter dedicated to the art of listening.

Ichigo ichie is a call to recover the power of attention, with your partner, friends, family, coworkers, society, and the whole world.

It involves being aware that this moment might be the last that returns us to the present, in the same way that we would listen intently to someone's dying words. And the image is no coincidence. Only when we are fully present with others can we truly receive everything they have to offer.

In a world full of conflicts, we need more than ever to stop navel gazing and become more connected to other people. Practicing attention and awareness together can save the world.

A New Kind of Mindfulness

Most mindfulness exercises are oriented toward practicing individual attention. Through trainings like the mindfulness-based stress reduction (MBSR) devised by Jon Kabat-Zinn, we learn to be aware of our body and our thoughts and emotions.

In this eight-week course, students learn to pay attention to their breathing and to each of their limbs. They are present when they rest, walk, and even when a cloud of negative thoughts invades their mental space.

How do we go from this individual attention and presence to a collective mindfulness? How can we move from our inner world, with our own perceptions, judgments, and needs, to the world of others, so we can share unique moments in a profound way?

According to Andrés Martín Asuero, a pioneer of mindfulness in Latin America and our MBSR teacher, paying attention to oneself immediately makes it easier to connect with others. As he explains in an interview, "The practice of mindfulness helps us realize what we do, how we do it, how we feel about what we do, and how others feel. And based on that knowledge, we can put procedures, mechanisms, and attitudes in place that are oriented toward harmony with oneself and with others."

Let's have a look at some strategies for strengthening this ability to pay attention to others.

- The first is common sense, which is why it's surprising that so few people actually do it: *Disconnect your devices when someone is talking to you.* It's humiliating trying to talk to someone who keeps glancing at their smartphone or even playing with it, a habit that betrays a lack of respect and can even be seen in the halls of government.

- *Listen to people's words and also to their body language.* People communicate how they feel about themselves and others through their gestures, posture, tone of voice, the look in their eyes. In this sense, complete attention means being aware of all this so that we can adjust to the other person's emotional state.

- *Ask questions without being intrusive.* Many people find it frustrating to explain something that's important to them—perhaps a problem they don't know how to resolve—and to be met with only silence and a pat on the shoulder. While we needn't offer solutions or take on a responsibility that isn't ours, a few thoughtful questions—along with the active listening we've already discussed—will be doubly beneficial to the person we're talking to. It shows that we're paying attention, and it could bring up aspects of the issue that might not have occurred to them.

- *Just be with people.* Often, what other people need isn't our opinion or even our questions. Some people need only company, and to know that we're there with them, sharing their pain or worries.

- *Or leave them in peace.* In high-stress situations, sometimes the best we can do for someone is to give them the gift of privacy. However urgent it may seem to resolve a conflict, if the other party is too worked up, they may benefit most from being left alone. Even if they're mad at us, the mindful approach can sometimes be to allow them to be angry and withdraw.

METTA BHAVANA

We are often unable to be in the moment because our mind is full of resentment and unfinished business with other people. And yet, as we saw at the beginning of this book, it's impossible to be in the past and the present at the same time.

How can we let go of hostile feelings toward people we believe have harmed us or treated us unfairly or who haven't reciprocated our love and friendship?

Metta bhavana is a five-stage Buddhist meditation that helps to calm the anger that removes us from the present moment and to transform negativity into love, understanding, and friendship.

To perform *metta bhavana*, which translates as "loving-kindness," you just need to follow these five steps:

1. Sit down and send feelings of warmth, kindness, and goodwill to yourself. Try to *feel* rather than *think* these emotions.

2. Now think about a friend, someone who isn't your partner or a relative, and try to summon even greater feelings of love toward this person.

3. Then think of a neutral person, someone about whom you feel indifferent, and focus on sending them feelings of fondness and humanity. Embrace their humanity.

4. Next, think about someone difficult or even an enemy, someone you dislike profoundly, and make an effort to summon that same feeling of warmth, goodwill, and understanding toward them.

5. To finish, bring these four people together in your mind—yourself, your friend, the neutral person, and the enemy—and try to harbor fond feelings for all four at once. Visualize this love spreading into your surroundings, your city, your country, and the whole world.

The World Is Invited

Directing your full attention to others isn't recommended only for conflict and pain. It's also useful in social settings, like those discussed in the previous chapter.

To see how this works in a celebratory context, we can look at the unique case of Jim Haynes, an American bohemian living in Paris, who at the time we finished writing this book was eighty-four years old.

Haynes, a countercultural activist, is a living legend in the French capital due to the popular "Sunday Dinners" he hosts in his Montparnasse studio, which is said to have belonged to Matisse. Anyone in the world can attend these dinners, which are *ichigo ichie* in nature, since the guests, all strangers, are unlikely to run into one another again.

To attend, you have to get Haynes's phone number and call to arrange to be part of the dinner, where a different Parisian chef cooks every Sunday (for free, because the social capital it confers is payment enough). The host's motto is "The world is invited."

People visiting from out of town pay a token amount for

food and drink, but the most interesting thing about these events is seeing Haynes in action, since the way he conducts the dinner is an example of collective mindfulness.

As they enjoy the different courses, the guests mill around browsing books on the shelves, some of which are by Haynes—like *Workers of the World, Unite and Stop Working!* and *Thanks for Coming! An Autobiography*—and are published by his own company, Handshake Editions. At the time of our visit, he was planning to write a new book, *Cooking for a Hundred.*

Let's look at the full attention the host gives to everything that happens at these unique dinners for strangers. Standing on a stool, Haynes observes the distracted or solitary people in his studio and gives instructions on who should talk to whom.

A few examples might be as follows:

"You in the yellow sweater! Put that book down and go talk to the girl in glasses sitting on the couch."

"You two over there, yes, you two. You've been talking for a while. I suggest you go talk to those two weird guys serving the tabbouleh."

"There's a Japanese woman falling asleep under the lamp. Isn't anyone going to talk to her?"

The fundamental idea is for no one to feel left out.

From his stool, Haynes devotes his full attention to the people before him, bringing a touch of mindfulness to the art of introducing strangers to one another. According to the types and attitudes he perceives, he pairs people off to converse. More than one marriage or lifelong friendship has resulted from these dinners, which provide an antidote to the Sunday blues.

This champion of introductions, who has spent over three decades creating *ichigo ichie* every Sunday, seems to channel the philosophy of the famous poem written by John Donne in 1624:

> No man is an island entire of itself; every
> man is a piece of the continent, a part of the
> main; if a clod be washed away by the sea,
> Europe is the less, as well as if a promontory
> were, as well as any manor of thy friends
> or of thine own were . . .

Returning to Now

In the chapter about Steve Jobs and Buddhism, we mentioned metacognition, our ability to examine our own minds. The founder of Apple practiced this, sitting in a zazen position facing a wall.

But there is no need to strain your back by sitting on a meditation cushion, or to be inspired by a Zen master, in order to observe your thoughts. It's enough to sit down in a quiet place and observe what flits across your mental screen without judging it at any point.

What we are doing is shifting the focus of our attention inward and asking ourselves, "What am I thinking?"

If we observe with detachment, we'll see memories,

ideas, pleasant or disturbing emotions, beliefs, rational or absurd thoughts as they pass through our mind.

Even if what appears on your inner screen is an aberration, your attitude should be neutral, lest you stray from the assumption that "You are not your thoughts." When we separate the observer from the observed in this metacognition exercise, we manage to detach ourselves from our mind at the same time we observe its processes. This helps us reach a state of calm.

When we stop identifying ourselves with our thoughts, our ego dissolves and we flow fully with the moment, at the same time deeply and intuitively understanding the nature of reality. These moments of epiphany are a solitary *ichigo ichie*, moments of such lucidity that they encompass a whole life.

MAHARSHI'S ANSWER

In an article about Advaita—the mystical experience of unity that is present in the origins of Hinduism— the essayist Anna Sólyom recalls an encounter between the spiritual teacher Papaji and Sri Maharshi in 1944. The young Papaji asked the great Indian master a question he had asked all the gurus and holy people he had met during his long spiritual quest:

"Can you show me God? And if not, do you know of anyone who can?"

"I can't show you God, or allow you to see God," Maharshi answered, "because God is not an object that can be seen. God is the subject. He is the seer. Don't worry yourself about objects that can be seen. Find out who is the seer."

Instead of giving him a view of God, Maharshi guided Papaji toward his own being, making the observer fuse with the observed, just like in quantum physics. That was the beginning of Papaji's enlightenment.

Enemies of *Ichigo Ichie*

As we approach *satori*, the Zen vision of enlightenment that is completely tied to the moment, let's pause to identify the enemies of the present, the habits and attitudes that rob us of the gift of now, preventing us from experiencing unforgettable moments.

- *Projections.* As we have seen in the first part of this book, when our mind travels into the past, where pain and resentment reside, or the future, a place of fear and worries, we are pulled away from the present moment.

- *Distractions.* We can experience the present fully only if we aren't trying to do several things at once. A man strolling through the forest and updating social media on his phone is not living in the moment. In fact, he's not even in the forest.

- *Fatigue.* Getting a bad night's sleep or being overworked can get in the way of our enjoyment of the present moment. In the first case, because we're in the grip of tiredness. In the second, because we're so mentally active that we can't reduce our level of stimulation enough to live in the present. A simple example is when we rush out of the office to go to a movie, but once we're seated, we can't focus on what's happening in front of us because the problems we've been grappling with are still flying around in our head.

- *Impatience*. Wanting to make things happen—for example, a lover who can't wait for the first kiss— also removes us from the present. *Ichigo ichie* demands that we give ourselves over to what we experience without any kind of expectation. Whatever is happening is the best we can experience, because we are experiencing it now.

- *Analysis*. There is a common saying that goes, "If you want to be happy, don't analyze everything." When we try to dissect the moment, we're in danger of killing it. Why must we search for the meaning of everything? Wanting to understand why what we're experiencing makes us happy immediately ruins that happiness. The joy of the moment can't be defined, dissected, understood; it can only be lived.

When Time Stands Still

Has it ever happened, in the middle of an activity you enjoy, that you felt like time no longer had any meaning? Just like when we dive into water and the only thing we feel is our body entering the coolness of another element, when we experience flow with an activity that absorbs us, we find ourselves mentally outside of time.

Albert Einstein explained it this way when asked about the relativity of time: "Put your hand on a hot stove for a minute and it seems like an hour. Sit with a pretty girl for an hour and it seems like a minute. That's relativity."

In fact, every *ichigo ichie* moment situates us in timelessness. It becomes meaningless to measure time because, as in Einstein's example, an hour can seem like a second, yet despite this, the memory of an experience can persist for days. Sometimes it can last a lifetime.

This happens because when we experience flow—when we flow completely with life—we step into timelessness. Not only time but also the whole world seems to disappear.

We find ourselves close to the *kenshō* and *satori* that we will now examine.

Satori According to D. T. Suzuki

In Zen Buddhism, when the present takes hold of our entire being, turning the past and the future and the physical world into an illusion, we are considered to have reached *satori*.

This state of momentary enlightenment, which sometimes arrives completely unexpectedly, is the ultimate goal of Zen practitioners: to capture a moment that contains all the beauty and understanding in the universe.

Daisetsu* Teitaro Suzuki is responsible for bringing Zen to the United States. He published the first books in English that made this branch of Japanese Buddhism accessible to Americans.

Suzuki eschewed the paraphernalia of other schools of Buddhism, with their symbols, rituals, and sacred texts, maintaining that, "To be immersed in Zen, you

---

* A title meaning "great simplicity," conferred on him by his Zen master Soyen Shaku.

just need to focus on your breath, on a movement, or on an unchanging landscape like a blank wall."

For Suzuki, *satori*, the sudden enlightenment sought by Zen practitioners, has the following characteristics:

1. *It's irrational.* It can't be reached through logic, since it challenges any kind of intellectual reasoning. Those who have experienced *satori* can't explain it in a coherent or logical way.
2. *It's intuitive. Satori* can't be explained, only lived and felt.
3. *It's direct and personal.* It's a perception that emerges from the innermost part of consciousness.
4. *It's an affirmation of life.* It implies acceptance of all that exists, of all things as they emerge, independent of their moral value.
5. *It gives us a sense of the beyond.* When we experience *satori*, we sense that it is rooted somewhere else. The hard individual shell encasing one's personality shatters the moment we experience *satori*. The feeling that follows is one of complete liberation or complete rest, of finally having arrived at one's destination.

6. *It has an impersonal tone.* In Suzuki's words, "Perhaps the most remarkable aspect of the Zen experience is that it has no personal note in it, as is observable in Christian mystic experiences."

7. *Feeling of exaltation.* Upon breaking with the restriction of being an individual, we experience an infinite expansion of our being.

8. *Momentariness.* "*Satori* comes upon one abruptly," Suzuki maintains, "and is a momentary experience, in fact, if it is not abrupt and momentary, it is not *satori*."*

SATORI AND *KENSHŌ*

Satori, which literally means "understanding," is the word used in Zen to refer to a kind of awakening or enlightenment. Another term used in Japanese Buddhism to refer to a state of enlightenment is *kenshō.*

---

* Summarized in his book *Zen Buddhism: Selected Writings of D. T. Suzuki* (New York: Anchor Books, 1956), 103–8.

The differences between *kenshō* and *satori* have been discussed extensively by various authors. According to Suzuki, *kenshō* is a momentary experience in which you see your own nature through a direct tunnel, while *satori* is a deeper and more lasting transformation.

Both of these states can be reached by our consciousness to connect with the present and our true nature, which is to become one with the universe rather than being caught up in anxiety.

Even if we don't reach these states of enlightenment, we can approach them through practicing any kind of meditation.

Zen Meditation

We have both practiced different kinds of meditation throughout our lives: zazen, mindfulness, and *metta bhavana*, among others. We have no preference for any specific kind, having found all of them to be effective tools for living more in the present.

If you are new to these practices, find the one that suits you best and that makes you feel good. At first it might be useful to have someone supervise your physical position and address any doubts that might come up. Eventually, you can incorporate meditation into your daily routine without any outside help.

For those with anxiety, there are mindfulness apps that you can use to meditate, even if only for five minutes a day.

The following classic Zen meditation can be practiced anywhere. All it takes is twenty minutes a day to see enormous progress in your level of serenity and in your ability to capture the moment.

1. Sit in a peaceful spot, where no one can bother you. You can use a meditation cushion or a simple chair. Sit comfortably, with your back straight.

2. Focus all your attention on the air that slowly enters and leaves your nostrils. Give all your attention to this life-giving process.

3. To help you concentrate, you can count your breaths in groups of ten. If you lose track at any

point, or if a thought pulls you into the past or the future, start counting over again.

4. Don't worry if, while you meditate, all kinds of thoughts come into your mind. Think of them as clouds floating by. Remember that you are not your thoughts. Let them pass by without judging them.

5. If during the meditation you manage to keep your mind free of thoughts for only a few seconds, consider this a success. After your meditation session, you'll feel as rested as if you'd been asleep for hours.

6. Don't transition too quickly from meditation to activity. After you finish your session, give yourself time to stretch and move your body before going back to your other activities.

What If . . . ?

One of the novels that has given us the most food for thought is *The Magus*, which took its author, John Fowles, twenty years to write. It tells the story of Nicholas, a young man bored with his life in London, who accepts a job as an English teacher on a remote Greek island.

There he meets a mysterious character, an eccentric millionaire named Conchis—the magus of the title—who turns every encounter into a game in which the borders between dreams and reality become blurred.

When we read this novel, both of us agreed that the magus is motivated to create these outlandish scenarios by the island's despondent atmosphere in the hope of pushing the limits of the predictable.

The following saying applies: "If you don't like reality, create another where you can live." Each of us has heeded this advice several times, leading to radical changes in where we lived, several career changes, and the investigation of remote places like the village on the Japanese island of Okinawa that inspired our book *Ikigai*.

A Magical Question

Just as we give children colored pencils so they can make new worlds spring from blank paper, adults, too, can create different realities to escape from tedium.

Everyone has a creative muscle. It's just that some people use it and others don't.

Some people believe they aren't creative. But this isn't really true for anyone; human beings are made to adapt, invent, learn, transform, and be transformed. The life of any human is a constant act of creation, from the moment we're born.

When we're bored and feel like the spark has gone out of life, we can turn to a magical question that the Italian writer and educator Gianni Rodari considered the philosopher's stone.

The question to ask, as much to write a story as to write—or reinvent—the script of your life, is

What if . . . ?

When we ask this question, we open the floodgates to the creative flow we need to unblock ourselves and step into a world full of *ichigo ichie*. Let's look at some examples of how to use this question in three situations that often make people feel indifferent to life.

1. *I've been bored by my job for a while and don't know what to do.* What would happen if I took a leave of absence or saved enough to live on for a few months and allowed myself to explore other possibilities?

2. *My partner and I are constantly arguing. Sometimes we even avoid speaking to each other so that we don't have to fight.* What would happen if we played the game Island of Harmony, which challenges you

not to think or say anything negative—either to complain or to rebuke each other—for as long as the session lasts?

3. *I'm having a crisis; I feel unsatisfied with my life, but I don't know why.* What would happen if I allowed myself to be someone else, or even many other people, for the next few months?

As soon as we transform our malaise into the question "What if . . . ?," we trade paralysis for movement, because thinking up creative hypotheses for our lives is the first step toward making change a reality.

What if, after reading this book, you made real changes to the way you live? What would your life be like then?

The *Ichigo Ichie* Formula

We have reached the end of this book. We hope it will serve as inspiration for you to enjoy many unforgettable moments with those most important to you, beginning with yourself.

We began our adventure in an old teahouse in Kyoto, reading, as the master Ikkyū said, the love letters sent by the wind and rain. A *sakura* blossom from that spring will help us synthesize the formula for *ichigo ichie*, using the ingredients we have seen throughout these pages.

If we are moved by a celebration like the *chanoyu*, it will remain engraved in our hearts. As Maya Angelou said, "People will forget what you said, people will forget

what you did, but people will never forget how you made them feel."

To live these words, we must become masters of ceremonies in our own lives, giving meaning to every moment, creating in the here and now the things that will feed our nostalgia in the future. To do so, just like Scott Matthew sings in one of our favorite songs, "Make it beautiful now!"

Good company is also essential for *ichigo ichie*, since

people with no *joie de vivre* can ruin any party or gathering with their negativity. If you have the opportunity to choose, surround yourself with happy, inspiring people who are capable of valuing and sharing the beauty of every moment, and who have the ability to listen.

If you find yourself alone, make sure you are good company! With the right spirit, a tea with yourself can be an unforgettable celebration.

Find an inspiring place to meet, since some places encourage the best feelings and conversations. A soulful café, a restaurant that reminds you of your childhood, a quiet street with the atmosphere of another era, a forest that caresses the senses with its poetry and fresh air.

You can also make your house, and even your workplace, a temple to *ichigo ichie*. Pleasant lighting—perhaps some candles in the evening—pictures and objects that evoke positive feelings, music to strike the right chord in your heart . . . If you know how to create the right wrapping, the present will be your gift.

Ichigo ichie depends on our ability to listen, see, touch, smell, and savor every moment, doing only one thing at a time, and putting our heart and soul into it, as if it were the last thing we were going to experience on Earth.

Timelessness will come by itself if we give ourselves over to the experience with the rest of the petals of this *sakura* blossom. A ritual that awakens the emotions in the best of company—even if it's just our own—in an inspiring setting, and with the right frame of mind, will make us flow, and in that flow, yesterday and tomorrow will disappear, and we'll feel time stand still in an ongoing present. Perhaps we will even experience *satori*.

To make this happen, we need to put our watches and cell phones away. The moment is a jealous lover that demands we give it our all.

Every unrepeatable moment is a small oasis of happiness.

And many oases together make an ocean of happiness.

Epilogue:
The Ten Rules of *Ichigo Ichie*

We'll conclude our ceremony together in these pages with ten principles that sum up the philosophy we've learned in this book.

1. **Don't postpone special moments.** Like the hunter in the story at the beginning of the book who finds the gate to Shambhala open, each opportunity presents itself only once. If you don't embrace it, it's lost forever. Life is a question of now or never.

2. **Live as if this were going to happen only once in your life.** The advice given by the tea master half a millennium ago still holds. That's why it's

inspiring to greet and say goodbye to our loved ones with "*Ichigo ichie*," to make us aware of the unique and once-in-a-lifetime nature of each meeting.

3. **Dwell in the present.** Journeys into the past and the future are often painful and nearly always useless. You can't change what happened. You can't know what will happen. But here in this moment, all the possibilities in the world are alive.

4. **Do something you've never done before.** As Einstein said, you can't do the same thing over and over and expect different results. Another way of achieving an unforgettable moment is by giving yourself over to *kaika* and allowing something new to blossom inside you.

5. **Practice zazen.** You can sit on a meditation cushion or just sit down and observe the miracle of life. The simple fact of stepping away from the daily whirlwind of hurry and obligations will open the doors to well-being.

6. **Apply mindfulness to your five senses.** Train yourself in the art of listening, watching, touching,

tasting, and smelling to give each moment the richness of human perception. This will also allow you to be more alert to others and increase your level of empathy and influence.

7. **Notice coincidences.** Being aware of coincidences helps us get better at reading signs sent by the universe. A journal in which we keep notes of these moments of daily magic will increase our ability to follow the invisible threads of reality.

8. **Make every gathering a party.** Don't wait for the right circumstances—a vacation, a trip, a birthday—to experience extraordinary things. With the right frame of mind, every day can be a celebration.

9. **If you don't like what there is, make something different.** Human beings are transformative by nature and have the power to reinvent themselves as many times as it takes. If your reality is too dull and predictable to live with *ichigo ichie*, you have the opportunity to create another.

10. **Be a hunter of special moments.** Like with any activity, the more you practice, the better and more abundant the results will be.

Thank you for coming this far with us. This is just the beginning. When you close this book, you will open your life, where many unforgettable moments await you. *Ichigo ichie!*

Héctor García and Francesc Miralles

ACKNOWLEDGMENTS

Thanks to John Siciliano, Gretchen Schmid, and the wonderful team at Penguin for loving this book as much as we do.

Thanks to Anna Sólyom for her support throughout the process of writing this book, and for being our first reader.

Thanks to Ana Gázquez, who shared her discoveries about human perception from her Canadian Fargo.

Thanks to Cristina Benito, master of ceremonies for our London presentation; to our "bro" Andrés Pascual for his advice, and for providing accommodation at his Notting Hill apartment.

Thanks to Maria White, Joe Lewis, and Patrick Collman, who contributed their talents to showing the world this project.

Thanks to our talented agents, Sandra and Berta Bruna, and to all of their coagents, for taking our books to every corner of the world.

And thanks to our readers all over the world, who give our work meaning and motivation.

SUGGESTIONS FOR FURTHER READING

Anonymous. *The Tale of the Heike*. New York: Penguin, 2012.

Auster, Paul. *The Red Notebook: True Stories*. New York: New Directions, 1992.

Chino Otogawa, Kobun. *Embracing Mind: The Zen Talks of Kobun Chino Otogawa*. Los Gatos, CA: Jikoji Zen Center, 2016.

Cyrulnik, Boris. *Resilience: How Your Inner Strength Can Set You Free from the Past*. London: Penguin, 2009.

Donne, John. *The Complete English Poems*. New York: Penguin, 2017.

Fowles, John. *The Magus*. Boston: Little, Brown, 2012.

Gladwell, Malcolm. *Outliers: The Story of Success*. Boston: Little, Brown, 2008.

Jung, Carl. *Synchronicity: An Acausal Connecting Principle*, Jung Extracts, Book 8. Princeton, NJ: Princeton University Press, 2010.

Kabat-Zinn, Jon. *Full Catastrophe Living: Using the Wisdom of Your Body and Mind to Face Stress, Pain, and Illness.* New York: Random House, 2009.

Kakuzo, Okakura. *The Book of Tea.* New York: Penguin, 2016.

Lindahl, Kay. *The Sacred Art of Listening: Forty Reflections for Cultivating a Spiritual Practice.* Nashville: Skylight Paths, 2001.

Lorenz, Edward Norton. *The Essence of Chaos.* Seattle: University of Washington Press, 1995.

Nhat Hanh, Thich. *The Miracle of Mindfulness: A Manual on Meditation.* Boston: Beacon Press, 1996.

Proust, Marcel. *Swann's Way.* New York: Penguin Books, 2002, trans. Lydia Davis.

Rodari, Gianni. *The Grammar of Fantasy: An Introduction to the Art of Inventing Stories.* New York: Teachers & Writers Collaborative, 1996.

Suzuki, D. T. *Zen Buddhism: Selected Writings of D. T. Suzuki.* New York: Doubleday, 2018.

Zimbardo, Philip, and John Boyd. *The Time Paradox: The New Psychology of Time That Will Change Your Life.* New York: Simon & Schuster, 2008.